WARRIOR
OF
LIGHT

KEVIN HUNTER

WARRIOR
OF
LIGHT

*Messages from my
Guides and Angels*

KEVIN HUNTER

BALBOA
PRESS

A DIVISION OF HAY HOUSE

Balboa Press books may be ordered through booksellers or by contacting:

Balboa Press
A Division of Hay House
1663 Liberty Drive
Bloomington, IN 47403
www.balboapress.com
1-(877) 407-4847

www.kevin-hunter.com

PRODUCTION CREDITS:
Project Editor: James Szopo
Author interior photo by photographer, Edwin Santiago
http://www.edwinsantiago.com/

Because of the dynamic nature of the Internet, any web addresses or links contained in this book may have changed since publication and may no longer be valid. The views expressed in this work are solely those of the author and do not necessarily reflect the views of the publisher, and the publisher hereby disclaims any responsibility for them.

The author of this book does not dispense medical advice or prescribe the use of any technique as a form of treatment for physical, emotional, or medical problems without the advice of a physician, either directly or indirectly. The intent of the author is only to offer information of a general nature to help you in your quest for emotional and spiritual well-being. In the event you use any of the information in this book for yourself, which is your constitutional right, the author and the publisher assume no responsibility for your actions.

Any people depicted in stock imagery provided by Thinkstock are models, and such images are being used for illustrative purposes only.
Certain stock imagery © Thinkstock.

Printed in the United States of America.

ISBN: 978-1-4525-7419-6 (sc)
ISBN: 978-1-4525-7418-9 (e)

Balboa Press rev. date: 05/20/2013

Acknowledgements

Thank you to my spiritual posse that consists of God and my personal sports team of Angels, Guides, Archangels and Saints. Thank you to Archangel Michael, Archangel Gabriel, Archangel Uriel and the leader of my pack, Saint Nathaniel (who sometimes refers to himself as Bartholomew). If it were not for all of you this book would not be possible or have come to light.

Dedication

If you have this book in your hand, then that is because you were guided to it by your own Spirit team in Heaven. This is for all of you in order to help change humanity towards a brighter new world.

A Word

"It does not matter if you are a believer or a skeptic, because your team of Guides and Angels believe in you regardless. They are always there illuminating the path on your journey. They are guiding you out of despair and towards peace, love and joy throughout your Earthly life. All you need to do is pay attention to their messages and signs."

—Kevin Hunter

Contents

Author's Note

Warrior of Light: Messages from my Guides and Angels is infused with practical messages and guidance that my Spirit team has taught and shared with me revolving around many different topics. The main goal is to fine tune yourself, which subsequently improves humanity at the same time. You are all Divine communicators and perfectly adjusted and capable of receiving messages from Heaven. This is for your benefit in order to live a happier, richer life. It is our individual responsibility to respect ourselves and this planet while on our journey here. The messages and information enclosed in this book may be in my own words, but they do not come from me. They come from God, the Holy Spirit, my Spirit team of guides, angels and sometimes certain Archangels and Saints. I am merely the liaison or messenger in delivering and interpreting the intentions of what they wish to communicate. They love that I talk about them and share this stuff as it gets other people to work with them too. There is one main hierarchy Saint who works with me leading the pack. His name is Nathaniel. He is often brutally truthful and forceful, as he does not mince words. There may be topics in this book that might bother you or make you uncomfortable. He asks that you examine the underlying cause of this discomfort and come to terms with the fear that is attached to it. He cuts right to the heart of humanity without apology. I have learned quite a bit from him while adopting his ideology, which is Heaven's as a whole.

I am one with the Holy Spirit and have many Spirit Guides and Angels around me. As my connections to the other side grew to be daily over the course of my life, more of them joined in behind the others. I have often seen, sensed, heard and been privy to the dozens of magnificent lights that crowd around me on occasion. If I use the word "He" when pertaining to God, this does not mean that I am advocating that he is a male. Simply replace the word, "He" with one you are comfortable using to identify God for you to be. This goes for any gender I use as examples. When I say, "spirit team", I am referring to a team of 'Guides and Angels'. The purpose of "Warrior of Light" is to empower you and help you to improve yourself, your life and humanity as a whole. It does not matter if you are a beginner or well versed in the subject matter. There may be something in this that reminds you of something you already know or something that you were unaware of. We all have much to share with one another, as we are all one in the end. "Warrior of Light" contains information and directions on how to reach the place where you can be a fine tuned instrument to receive your own messages from your own Spirit team.

Some of my personal stories are infused in this in order for you to live vicariously through osmosis on how it works effectively for me. With some of my methods I hope that you gain insight, knowledge or inspiration out of it. It may prompt you to recall incidents where you were receiving divine messages in your own life. There are helpful ways that you can improve your existence and have a connection with Heaven throughout this book. Doing so will greatly transform yourself in all ways allowing you to attract wonderful circumstances at higher levels and live a happier more content life.

—Kevin Hunter

WARRIOR OF LIGHT

*Messages from my
Guides and Angels*

Chapter One

SPIRIT GUIDES AND ANGELS

HOW OFTEN DO YOU FIND yourself thinking about nothing in particular when suddenly a jolt of clear-cut information flies through your mind? What you receive is so commanding you experience a surge of uplifting joy coursing through all of the cells in your body. The idea, key or answer you gained was the missing piece of the puzzle to something you needed to know at that particular time. How many times have you received a nudge to do something that would positively change your life? Instead of taking action on it you deny it chalking it off to wishful thinking. You later discover that it was indeed an answered prayer if only you had taken notice and followed it. These are some examples of how you can tell that it is your Spirit Guide or Guardian Angel communicating with you. When you get yourself and your Ego out of the way, then that is when the profound answer you had been hoping for is revealed to you. The impression you acquire is so powerful that it pulls you out of the darkness you were previously stuck in. It is a bright light shining its focus directly onto the message in unadorned view. It is crystal clear as if it had been there all along and you wonder why you had not noticed it before.

There are so many joyless faces out there waiting, complaining or praying for a miracle. What you are looking for is right in front of you and closer than you think when you have faith and believe. Instead, we choose to go through our days partaking in activities that only erode our self-esteem and overall well-being. These are things you are not even aware of like sitting in traffic completely tense. We experience another mundane routine day screaming for an escape from this prison of a life we have created. We stay unhappy in our jobs, the places we live in and with certain friendships or relationships. We ponder over not having that home of our dreams or sharing our life with someone in a loving relationship. The days having this dull mindset turn into months and years with no miracle in sight. This disappointment grows causing you to appear eternally glum, negative and bitter. Those emotional traits mask your disappointment and heartbreak attracting more of that to you. To cope you drown those nasty emotions with addictions from drinking heavily, ingesting chemicals, doing drugs or by partaking in time wasting activities such as gossip and Internet surfing. We choose to be disconnected living behind a wall built of our own attitude and yet it is in our basic human nature to want to connect to other human souls, to someone or something. We all want to be happy, but that state can often feel so out of reach and unobtainable we drown in its thoughts.

Our way of communicating today is primarily through cell phone texting, email and social networking. Even if we truly wanted to sit face-to-face we are all too busy or worn out to bother. We were not intended to live our lives in misery and unhappiness. For some reason, we choose to fall into a pattern of suffering. We as a whole are to blame for this design. It is never too late to improve your life and God, your angels, guides and all in Heaven can and want to assist you out of this hopelessness. They are always right there next to you wanting to lift you out of your life of desolation. It does not matter what your beliefs are and whether you are religious or an atheist. It does not matter what your race is, whether you are rich or poor, gay or straight, liberal or conservative. Whatever you agreed to come into this lifetime as, you are all loved equally. No one is more special than anyone else. God and the angels see each of your inner lights, your innocence and your true purpose for being here. If you have veered long off course, they can help you get back to where you need to be. Who you are is a perfect child of God and love no matter where you are from or who you are.

WHAT ARE SPIRIT GUIDES AND ANGELS?

A Spirit Guide once lived as human, but a Guardian Angel has always been a Spirit. Each of you has one Spirit Guide and one Guardian Angel assigned to work with you throughout your entire Earthly life. They are your immediate army that works with you daily from the moment you were born until you pass on to the next life. They know everything about you, from your thoughts and feelings to your wants and desires. Murderers, serial killers and those filled with hate towards others also have a Spirit Guide and Guardian Angel with them. Because we have Free Will choice those people are not listening to or following the guidance that is passed onto them by their Spirit team. Some of you have more than one Spirit Guide and one Guardian Angel if you have been requesting additional assistance from Heaven or you are working with angels regularly. These Guides and Angels are attracted to your light and know if you are an honorable person by how greatly your light shines. When this happens, then more Guides and Angels may come to your side. They know you are one with Heaven and are excited to work with you and help you along your journey.

Your Spirit team does not make your choices for you. They work with you to help you along with your growth and to keep you on the right path. They assist in orchestrating circumstances that will improve your life at the right time. This can include coming into contact with particular people on Earth to help enhance your life in some way or to teach you certain lessons. You can call on your team to assist you anytime. You do have to ask for their assistance because they cannot intervene with our Free Will. They may stand idly by while you make one mistake after another. They are unable to interfere with your poor choices unless you have asked them to or permanently invited them in.

They will attempt to get your attention if you are heading off your path, but they cannot stop you. They know that these mistakes are essential to your spiritual growth. When you keep making mistakes and bad things continuously happen to you, then it hopefully gets you to notice this negative synchronistic pattern and find another path. They hope that it will wake you up to finally say, "Wait a minute. What am I doing? Obviously the way I have been living has not been entirely successful. Guides and Angels I call upon you now. Please work with me and assist me on my path and help me to reach a place of peace. Thank you."

We are always receiving Angel and Guide communication, messages and nudges, but are you paying attention to them? More people than not believe in angels regardless of what their spiritual beliefs are. God, Heaven and the Angels are all non-denominational. This means that they do not belong to any religious sect. You can be a non-believer and they are still with you, working with you and guiding you on your path. Your Spirit Guide and Guardian Angel are both with you from the time you are born until you exit this life. Your Spirit Guide is typically a deceased relative, but not always. This deceased relative is one who has chosen to be your Spirit Guide before you were born. It can even be a relative from centuries back. This Spirit Guide has gone through formal training to be able to efficiently guide you knowing when not to interfere allowing you your Free Will choice. If they see that you are a danger to yourself or someone else they will tap you on the shoulder and attempt to divert or talk you out of it.

Let's say that you decide to head over to someone's house to do drugs all night. Your Spirit Guide will nudge you to head down another course. Your Ego is so strong and powerful that it will convince you that you will be happier if you go into that house and get high. What might end up happening can be a circumstance that propels you into the bell jar. An array of negative activity can follow such as you experience an overdose, someone steals your wallet, something medically goes wrong or you have an accident. Perhaps you lose your job, a friendship, relationship or any other incident that thrusts your life into a downward spiral preceding that night. From this one incident you attract in more of the same causing you to experience one detriment after another further delaying your purpose. Your Spirit Guide cannot stop you, but they are communicating with you in an attempt to get you to notice a different life choice that will not have such negative repercussions. This is the extent of the intervention since they are not allowed to stop you from doing that drug unless it results in death before your time. There are cases where unfortunately your guide did all they can do and were unable to divert you from continued bad behavior. You were not paying attention to them and were consumed in pain, greed or rebelliousness, which results in your early death.

Your Spirit Guide and Guardian Angel may alternate with specific roles in helping you. When you are down or depressed, your Guardian Angel may be the one that tries to get your attention to focus on the bright side of life. They will caress and soothe your heart Chakra working on relieving you of the heavy burden you might be feeling. Your Guardian Angel will often be the one that works with you on your feelings of well-being, prompting you to be more optimistic and joyful. Whereas your Spirit Guide may be working on more practical matters that lead you to that career you always wanted. Your Spirit Guide may direct you to take certain classes in the area of your dream making sure you stick to it. They will then guide you to the job they feel is beneficial for you at that time, even if it's not quite the job you always wanted. Sometimes you have to go through your own individual training and lessons with several different jobs before you are shown the big dream job. They do not give you anything immediately necessarily, but they rather gradually guide you towards your dream goal in steps.

You could be someone who has spent years looking for a job only to be met with dissatisfaction that there is no work out there. There may be situations where there are no jobs in the area you are looking in. What you might not be seeing is that you are being guided to a job, but it is not the job you want. You are being expected to start somewhere even in a position you do not want. You may be asked to take a position that you feel is beneath you or for less pay. I have done this myself only to find that it leads directly to the dream position I do want. I am suddenly catapulted upward to one of the greatest jobs I would have had to date. You need to have faith that there is a divine plan for you.

All those in Heaven are present in this Earthly life to make our lives easier, but the catch is that you have to ask them for help as they cannot intervene without your consent. The only time they do intercede is when there is a life-threatening situation before it's your time to go. This is God's law as he gave us all Egos and Free Will. Ego and Free Will are the biggest cause of turmoil, hate and destruction known to man. We are given Free Will choice to either live in peace or live stressed out. Which one would you like to have? You can have more peace and joy in your life when you start paying attention to your Spirit team's guidance. They do not live our lives for us because we are all here to learn and grow, but they do assist us in navigating gracefully out of circumstances that consistently cause us grief, stress and depression. They do not want us to suffer, but we must all learn valuable lessons while here.

I made great strides and shifts from living under duress with a wide range of addictions to living more at peace by working with my Spirit team. I discovered that the angels around each of us could help you improve yourself from having more time available, to getting more exercise, or to finding the right job. For some things the change is immediate and for bigger needs it may take much longer. This is because there are pieces of the puzzle that they must maneuver around on your behalf. You may not be quite ready and have additional life lessons to learn before you graduate to the next step. Everything is all set according to divine timing, but if you do not ask your Spirit team for help, then they stand by watching you suffer. They watch you be needlessly miserable when all you need to do is call out to them. I liken it to the mythological stories about Vampires that state that a Vampire cannot enter your house unless you invite it in. The concept is similar to asking anyone in Heaven or the Spirit world for help or to work with you. They will stand outside your door waiting patiently for you to say the magic words and invite them into your life. It's like having a winning sports team on your side, as you cannot lose!

I have always believed in angels and have never questioned Heaven's existence. I do not falsely follow something without testing it out first or because someone tells me this is the way to go and the way it is. I have an analytical mind that questions everything and is suspicious of anything. When I receive proof or a response that validates what I'm questioning, then I become a believer. The reason I greatly believe in God, Heaven, the Angels and Spirit Guides is because I have been testing them my entire life. I have had immense feedback and success simply by paying attention to their Divine intervention and communication. I do not try to convince or convert anybody, but rather share information about them. I graciously part with some of the messages that they have shared with me in my life.

There are those who are deeply religious who have said that you're not supposed to pray to angels or archangels. I have never seen anyone including myself urge anyone to pray to the angels. Asking your guide and angels for assistance isn't praying to them. They are the gifts from God who are available to help when you need it. They are his arms and hands that connect us to God. When we are experiencing negative emotions or behavior then we are cut off from God. The angels, guides and archangels lift our vibration to the level of happiness so that we feel God's connection. Their role is to lift you to a happier state where you are at peace. This level is where you will feel God's presence and receive His communication. When you ask your Spirit team for help you are essentially reaching out to God.

Calling them and asking them for help is mandatory if you need assistance in your life. When you are upset or stressed not only do you not receive God's wisdom, but you forget to ask for help. All you have to do is ask, whether that be mentally, out loud or even in writing. I have even sent some of them an email. I send it to myself and then I file it away. You can write to them in a journal, notebook or a piece of paper. It doesn't matter how you ask for help, how you word it or say it as no special invocation is needed. They often come in to you before you have finished your sentence. It's having the intention to do so is what is important. For example, thinking something mentally such as: "Ok Archangel Michael, I need your help with this." He has already rushed in before you have finished your sentence. Sometimes they respond immediately in some form or if it's complicated it may take a bit longer. It is important to have faith and trust that they are and have indeed stepped in and are working with you on your concern. Sometimes they may respond in ways that you may not be noticing. After it has hit you a few times you may get that moment where you say, "Ok I thought something was going on with that." You must be open and receptive knowing that sometimes they may not answer you in the way you are expecting.

My mom taught me how to pray when I was a wee tike. Every night as I went to bed she would enter my room and say my prayers with me. We were not religious and there was not a shred of guilt, fear or damnation surrounding our prayers. My mom was all about compassion and love. Her goal was that we all grow up to be good people helping and contributing to the world in a positive way. We said these prayers every night. My mom was and is all compassion and love for all people regardless of their interests or lifestyle. Her mantra in these prayers was to practice and teach love while in this lifetime when we were young and when we grow up. She would walk me through communicating to Jesus, Mother Mary and Joseph. I never had the fear and guilt when connecting to Jesus specifically or Mother Mary. I did grow up to notice that others did not share these same beliefs. I had noticed that when I have used the words God, Heaven, Jesus or Mother Mary around certain people I could tell they would be fidgeting uncomfortably. Some of that is fear and guilt. They were raised to associate those words with those who speak of an angry, judgmental and negative God. I have never seen Jesus or Mother Mary in any other way than 'all love' even if others disagreed. It is important to not be or feel led by man's Ego. They insist on creating this fear that there is a merciless Heaven that will cast you out into fire and brimstone at any moment. God will never cease to love you, but he does expect you to correct your mistakes and behavior if it is delaying you on your path or hurting yourself or someone else.

We all have a life purpose and mission to accomplish while we are here and it is our goal to discover what that is individually. Everyone needs to be contributing something in a positive way that is bringing love to another person. We were not born here angry, bitter and depressed. Others have inflicted that on us and we absorbed it and reacted to it in ways where it had might have permanently damaged us. Everything can be reversed and will be undone in this life or in the next when you pray and ask for heavenly assistance. Invite them to work with you on improving your life. They love you and want you to live in peace.

How Do Guides and Angels Communicate With Us?

Those in the spiritual realm that work with and communicate with us are angels, guides, archangels; spirit guides, guardian angels, saints, ascended masters and deceased loved ones. Since they cannot just pick up the phone and call you, they use other varying means and methods to communicate with you called *clairs*. Your senses are actually divine communication tools with Heaven! This is why your senses, Chakras and over all well-being needs to be kept clean of debris and trash that blocks the communication line with God. The more negative you are, then the more clogged your *clairs* get. This is why spiritual practitioners insist on living as joyful and toxic free of a life as you can manage.

There are four basic Clairs:

- » Clairvoyance (clear seeing)
- » Clairaudience (clear hearing)
- » Clairsentience (clear feeling)
- » Claircognizance (clear knowing)

You are all born with naturally heightened clear channels of communication to the other side. There are stories of children talking to or about angels or friends that cannot be seen. Unfortunately, as adults we often thrash and shatter that belief in those children by saying, "Oh that's just your imaginary friend." While you are born with all four clairs, there are typically one or two clairs, which tend to be more dominant than the others in you. Over time your clair channels dim due to things like blocks created by society, the material world, domination of the Ego, negative substances and poor lifestyle choices. All of these things clog your clair channels preventing you from communicating or even knowing that you're receiving messages from Heaven.

I was born with Clairaudience. For as long as I can remember, I have heard voices in my left ear as guidance and messages. It's ironic that the voices of my Guides and Angels are as clear as if they are standing right next to me talking into an ear that has always been deafer than the other. When I was four years old, I remember my mom taking me to the Doctor several times for hearing check ups. She would later tell me that I wasn't responding to any of the tests in my left ear and they thought I might be fully deaf. Every so often there is a ringing in that ear that has been undetected by medical professionals to be of anything of concern or that is measured in anyway. I later learned that was my Spirit team downloading important and vital information for me that I would need to access at some point. I equate it to hooking up a flash drive to your computer and moving important files off of it and onto your hard drive for immediate access. At times I will hear a dial up internet sound in my inner ear as if it is trying to connect. Other times if the reception is not clear, it will sound as if I'm switching the channels on a radio station until I hear a clear song.

Music is and has always been my escape. I love music as I am a rocker after all, but that is the only area I prefer it loud. As a clairaudient, my inspiration and messages are carried on the notes of music. This is where I hear everything clearly. All other loud sounds and noises are intrusive and strictly shunned and forbidden around me. This includes things such as crowd noise, sirens, airplanes, trashcans banging, screaming of any kind. Unpleasant noises are incredibly heightened with me and therefore often uncomfortable. I hear footsteps around me or someone approaching me and I immediately know who is coming or what type of person they are. I figured I was just odd that I constantly fixated on what might be deemed an unimportant sound, but it is all part of having clairaudience.

I put my spark and passion into my writing projects. I hear the music and the rhythms and that is how my Guides communicate with me. I hear it in the notes, in the music, in people's conversations, in the line at the store and it inspires me. I tap into the waves of the ocean and the voices rush over that and through the white noise. The music translates and the verbal messages come through that inspiration and through the sound. I hear everything in the sounds, from people's voices to the patterns in people's footsteps. I can tell what people are up to from those sounds. At the time I thought I was just a spaz having an acute hearing ability to every sound that happens around me. This has always been the case since I was a little kid. I did not know until adulthood that there was an actual word for it called clairaudience.

One afternoon I was running late and I could not find my car keys anywhere. I started throwing everything around in a panic mentally shouting, "Where are my keys!" I huffed and puffed throwing items all over the place and shouted again, "Angels. Where are my keys?!" I heard a loud male voice in my left ear shout, "On your bed!!" Without hesitating or even thinking twice about it I charged to my bedroom and there were my keys on my bed sitting all alone. I grabbed them abruptly and as I headed out of the house towards my car I mentally kept telling my Spirit team, "Thank you. Thank you. Thank you." The angels are unfazed by your sudden upset. All they see is the love buried inside you. Of course this doesn't give one license to behave as I did, but as you work with them more, you are less hostile and more appreciative. They see the light within us and ignore the range of wasted emotions, because to them everything is all right.

As my interests in the spiritual crowd grew, I went to an all day spiritually based convention. While there, I had to give someone a cold reading in the audience. This wasn't a test, but an exercise using no divination tool such as oracle or tarot cards. I was reminded that I personally didn't need them even though part of me likes to consistently confirm what I am getting. This is where the angels reminded me once again as they do repeatedly with all of us, "TRUST." Having to do a cold read in a space with hundreds of people's energies around me while on little sleep was not my cup of tea. I wanted to bolt out of there at lightning speed and crawl back into bed. I knew there was no way out. I could feel my team pushing me out of my comfort zone. I needed a volunteer to participate in this exercise. A young girl who was sitting near me raised her hand and said she'll do the read with me. She pulled her chair to face me and closed her eyes. I reached my hand out around her head to feel the air pressure to pick up on her energy. I remembered that this is not about me. This is about this girl in front of me. I closed my eyes and took several deep breaths until I was relaxed.

I started calling in my guides and said, "Please get my Ego out of the way. This is about this girl right here. It is all about her, not me. If anyone would like to come through for her, please come forward now." I repeated it with my eyes still closed. I then waited in stillness for some communication in any form. I heard a male voice speak through my clairaudience channel. My Ego was naturally trying to make me second guess it. I opened my eyes and what I said stopped her. "There is a pleasant man who is around you right now and he says he is always with you. He is telling me that his name is Ralph. He is your grandfather. He has been working closely with you on your education and towards your life purpose." I stopped noticing her eyes were flooded with tears. She said that she is sixteen years old and in High School. I thought she was in her twenties as she had a mature look to her and carried herself confidently as an adult. She was at this conference alone. She said her Mother's Dad, her Grandfather, died when she was seven years old. She then said that his name was RALPH.

Most of the time you are getting accurate information and messages from your own Spirit team, but we discredit it or talk ourselves out of it being real. I heard a male voice clearly telling me his name for this young girl. I thought I was imagining it at first. I was thinking, "I don't know any Ralph. This is silly." I decided to trust in the communication I was getting and not second guess it. It may not mean anything to me, but it might mean something to someone else. I decided to bite the bullet and just tell the girl what I heard knowing that I might be wrong. This was an excellent case where I realized again that there are loved ones communicating with us in Heaven. This was a complete stranger whom I had never met or knew anything about and I told her about her deceased grandfather. I am not a working Medium, but what I did in that instance for that girl was what one would call Mediumship. This is something anyone can do if they work at it. I no longer doubt or second guess the messages I receive and nor do I worry if I make a mistake.

I am Claircognizant as well, which is similar to having a computer in the mind. I receive Divine information through my crown Chakra that later proves to be true. It is an answer to a topic or subject matter that I am not versed in. I have often had people say to me, "How did you know that was going to happen?" I would say, "I don't know. I just knew." Growing up when they would ask that question I would stare at them blankly not understanding. I didn't know how I knew. I know when someone is lying even if I do not mention it to them. I would typically keep it to myself unless it is something major that needs addressing. This information proves useful on occasion, but then there are certain things you don't want to know or wished you were naïve to. You know this information is given to you in order to protect you and save you time and potential heartache.

I know if someone is cheating on me or someone else. I've known things about someone from a first meeting and what they are like. I can tell immediately what role they would play in my life if any. Everyone I dated I had known at first glance that I would be with them soon or one day in the future. It would always later happen and come to fruition. There was no explanation for it and I never questioned it. My mind is always on, thinking and working. Sometimes I find it difficult to shut it off when I need it to. I had even asked my Doctor once if there was something I could take that would help me to stop thinking specifically at night. He laughed and said, "Unfortunately there isn't anything like that." It was something that I had to accept as a gift and use it to my advantage. Knowing things before they happened and not known how or why has saved my life in many great ways.

Information or guidance often comes to you when you are not trying to get it. When you try to receive guidance or hear messages, then that is when you block it. Your fear is that you won't get it or that it's wishful thinking and therefore you hear and receive nothing. Your Spirit team is still communicating with you, but your strong will to try and receive something often dims it. The underlying core reason is due to your fear or destructive, unhelpful self talk. Negative emotions block communication with the other side. You can ask the angels to remove the blocks that cut off the communication to them. Ask them to help you clearly hear, see, know and feel the messages they wish to relay to you.

I was talking with a group of people standing in a circle at a beach BBQ at a house. There were many huddles of people talking at this BBQ around my group too. As I was talking to them, I took one step back grabbing the bottle of wine behind me to my right. I proceeded to pour it into the glass of a woman who was in another huddle near my group. She jolted in shock and laughed into a shout, "I was just going to get more wine! Wait! How did you know that? Ok that was weird." I just shrugged and said, "I don't know. I just knew." I had no idea how I knew and I was not looking at the woman or facing her. Something had prompted me to turn, grab the wine and pour. Other examples of Claircognizance are when you know the answers to problems or topics you are not educated in, but yet you had the right answer that solved it when others were perplexed. People with an analytical mind tend to be claircognizant. They can be people such as a Scientist or Professor.

I have always been wise beyond my years. In High School, I was the boy who would sit up in the bleachers and one by one a different student would approach me to divulge their issues as if I were their own private counselor. They were from every different clique you could imagine; the nerd, the jock, the cheerleader, the techie, the bully and the bullied would all come up to me solo at varying intervals. I'd say a sentence or two to them and they would cry out with something along the lines of having been given relief. "God you always know just what to say!" They would often say things like, "It's as if you're this old soul who knows the answers to life and yet you're a teenager in High School. How do you know so much?" I had no idea how I knew anything since I was too busy surviving and running for my life at the time. I knew that I was different, but the majority appreciated this eccentricity. I rarely had an unsettling moment. I did not think of myself as being different just for knowing information, but it was the whole package. I did not follow the crowd and was uninterested in fads or being popular. I never thought of myself as a follower, I was always an independent leader in some way. I would be comfortable with being alone and did not have a desire to be fulfilled in a constant demanding need for attention. I did not care if anybody liked or did not like me. My goal was and has always been beyond that.

Clairvoyance is the most known Clair. We can all work on having all four clair channels regardless of having two dominant clairs. Once in awhile I see images and moving picture visuals in my mind. Those that have heightened clairvoyance see actual Spirits as if they are in front of them. Those spirits are not necessarily whole like you and I, but rather appear opaque or translucent. Other forms of clairvoyance can include prophetic dreams or visual images being shown to you through your Third Eye Chakra located between your eyebrows. These images can be of importance to someone's future whether it is a warning or something good coming into your life like a romantic partner or a great job. As a child I saw images of people that at times appeared scary. I remember seeing someone who looked very real leaving my room. My heart would beat faster not knowing who or what that was. The next minute I'm standing in front of my mother's bed in the dark. She's dead tired, "What is it?" I'd be unable to speak staring at another visual of someone under her bed smiling. I didn't know how to communicate to her that I was pretty sure I was seeing dead people. Instead I said, "There's someone in the house." She'd reply, "There's no one here. It's just your imagination." As a Claircognizant, I remember not buying her response, but chose to keep it all to myself from that point forward. I knew I wouldn't get anywhere trying to convince an adult of something that is real and not imaginary.

Clairvoyant messages delivered can come to us in many ways including in our dreams. I had a vivid dream where I was wandering through what appeared to be an upper scale mall that one might find in a fancy Las Vegas Hotel. I saw this Spirit in a long black robe high in the air in the distance. It had its robe hoodie over its skeleton head with hollow eyes. It looked like the "Day of the Dead" artwork that you see depicted in certain Mexican art. I spotted it and I mumbled, 'uh-oh'. This Spirit immediately saw me and looked right through me. He quickly flew in the air around the gorgeous gold fountain in the center of the mall and headed right towards me. I turned to run, but in dreams you don't always run, move or get far when being chased. I was unable to move and was painfully paralyzed. The Spirit landed in front of me and pulled out a long spear. He held it up and he stabbed me in the stomach with it. The pain was sharp and I sensed every bit of it as I jolted awake. The pain continued after I awoke and then evaporated to a good degree until I felt nothing. It reminded me of the horror movie, *"Nightmare on Elm Street"* where something happens in the dream and you take it out feeling it with you as you wake up.

I followed the dream with some quick Sage clearing of my space. I connected with my guides and discovered that it wasn't actually a demon spirit that I invited in. It was me! It was my fear that manifested that entity. The Spirit stabbed me in my stomach where your Sacral Chakra is. That's where your power lies. I had to figure out where I was giving my power away and to take it back. I had to stop with the Ego infested fears and worries as they were unfounded. I invoked a white light from the other side that took over that area in my body and the pain went away. I am no longer in fear. This clairvoyant example was not one that was showing me a crystal clear visual of what was to come or a vision of the past. Often times the messages you get through your channels may need to be deciphered or decoded. You might have to do a little detective work to discover what is being relayed to you.

Clairsentience is feeling the answers, messages and guidance. Do you ever just have a gut feeling or a hunch about something specific about to happen? You advise someone accordingly about it only to discover that it does end up coming true? Do you get a strong feeling of joy that you or someone else is on the right path and this ends up coming true as well? Do you get a fear of dread when walking in a room that someone is not of a high integrity and that turns out to be true? Those are some examples of clairsentients. This is 'clear feeling'. It is similar to being an Empath, but the difference is that an empath has sympathy for those around them while a clairsentient will feel the guidance and messages being relayed to them. An empath is more likely to be a clairsentient because half of the feeling ingredients are already there.

I have a good degree of Clairsentients. Having two to three dominate clairs is rare, but I might have gladly handed the clairsentients back. It can be draining always feeling and sensing everything and everyone around me. This was not always a good thing, because I sensed all of the bad and pending dooms too. I could not stand being so sensitive that when I was old enough I began drinking and later turned to drugs and other addictions. I reached for anything that would dull and turn it off for good. My clairsentients was so highly calibrated that it bounced off the Richter scale once the violence in my childhood kicked in. I found there was nothing positive about sensing every feeling that existed. It took me a good part of my life to see and use it as a gift.

REACHING FOR THE WARRIOR WITHIN

I've lived several lifetimes in one, growing up open to a wider variety of experiences than most people can handle. And many cannot handle some of the things I've partaken in. I discuss my rise to becoming a Warrior of Light in my previous book, *"Reaching for the Warrior Within"*. I grew up in an abusive household with a Father who was a violent and controlling bully. This led me to split off into many different people. It wasn't long before I was smoking cigarettes from age fifteen to twenty-five. I started drinking alcohol before I was 17 and by the time I was the legal drinking age of 21, I was already a full blown partying alcoholic. This then led me to heavy drug use from getting stoned daily with marijuana to cocaine and Methamphetamine use. I was involved with drug dealers and escort call girls in relationships. I was in one dysfunctional relationship after another where they all strayed at some point in the end. They were searching and dating around or were bathed in there own nasty addictions. Sometimes some of us have to get beat up a bit to get a little street smart. Once you have been in the darkness, then you can easily help others navigate out of it.

With the help of my Guides and Angels, they helped me dissolve my addictions. When I was 26, I had made a complete turn around and the energy I had previously put into grabbing hold of toxic vices I was soon putting into more healthful ways of living. My connections to the other side also opened up in miraculous ways when I went clean. I had studied nutrition and was health conscious and curious as a teenager. I also exercised regularly then, but the darker side of me and the lower self was running the bigger part of the show. The situation would entail me doing a line of cocaine and then chasing it with a glass of carrot juice. I lived in immeasurable degrees of good and bad, light and dark walking that fine line into both elements equally.

My earlier life was about survival and living in fear. I ran for shelter in a plethora of toxic poisonous addictions instead. They were harmful to my body, my psyche and well-being. There was always one bad circumstance after another going wrong. I gradually and quickly began to discover early on in my life that I was happier and more successful not partaking in those previous poor ways of living, but it took some time to get there. My Spirit team was always with me backing me up. They helped me obtain all of the jobs I ever wanted including the entertainment business and getting in front of the right people. It was like hitting many forks in the road where I was given a choice. I was clearly shown each choice down each road. One road was full of rocks and thorns and surrounded by drugs, alcohol and other toxic addictions including people. The other road was lit up with a bright light and a timeline of positive events headed out into the distance for me to see. It was pretty clear to me which road I should head down on. I was an intelligent young man, but breathing in constant pain. Despite hopping from the light road to the dark road on occasion, I knew I did not want to blow it. I knew what was being handed to me and that I had to receive it in the right spirit. I knew that if I put in the effort with what I was given, then I would be taken care of.

I have always been communicating with a team of Guides and Angels on the other side. We all have this ability, but for me personally it was as natural and fluid as you call a friend up on the phone. I dimmed the communication to them to a good degree as a teenager when I rebelled against authority and swam in a sea of addictions. With the constant assistance and guidance of my Spirit team, I cleaned up my act and made a commitment to Heaven. Although the demons live in me buried, I have quieted and tamed them down for some time. Today I live comfortably and happily in the Light. I love me more now than I did growing up and into my twenties. My whole life has been a series of phases that has led to the joy that I experience now. I haven't wasted one-minute in my life always changing, always evolving, gaining knowledge and life experience beyond someone who has lived 100 Earth years. The biggest phase was when I made this official spiritual transformation as described in my book, *"Reaching for the Warrior Within"*. It was a pivotal transition, almost like a graduation in a sense where my world became brighter, but there were significant life choices I had to make to get to that place. I did not do it alone as my Guides and Angels were always communicating with me and guiding me down the path I needed to be on.

I left one juncture of my life and entered blissfully into the next one with immense excitement. I could always listen to other people's stories, trials and tribulations without judgment and follow it with my input, which includes the wisdom, inspiration or healing words that Heaven has taught me over the years. Even while buried in my own addictions, I was still being fed the answers and guidance from my Spirit team. I had blocked much of it out from being high, drunk, full of anxiety or depressed. Addictions and negative feelings of any kind cause a block between yourself and your Spirit team. They are always communicating with you and nudging you along your path of course, but you are not in a state to receive their communication. You are ignoring them without realizing it until you get a smack in the back of the head to take notice of the danger you have been putting yourself in.

My work and communications with my Spirit team of Guides and Angels grew to be daily during my official spiritual transformation. Before that, it was randomly and whenever without effort, whereas afterwards I made a commitment to invite God and them into my life permanently. They were instrumental in working with me to remove anything that was holding me back as well as assisting me in adopting a new improved lifestyle and way of doing things. Because the changing that was taking place was on the extreme side to something better, this would mean that I could no longer be around certain people. This was similar to when I quit drugs in my early twenties. Even though I had stopped doing drugs, I still hung out at the homes of these drug dealers, hustlers, ex-cons and users. It was about two months after I stopped the drugs that I cut them all out as well. Not only could I no longer relate to them sober, but their energy was lost in the darkness and self-destruction. I was quickly moving onto a brighter path and had to eliminate it completely or my foot would always be on the wrong side of the road. I never questioned it as it was literally as if I was standing in front of an open golden door feeling excitement and anticipation. I turned around to see the drug users one last time in their disintegrating dark hell environment. I smiled and waved goodbye. There were truly greener pastures, a rainbow and a pot of gold shining at the end of that yellow brick road I headed down instead. That was more attractive than the previous life I was living and there was no way I could deny it.

Chapter Two

HELL AND THE DEVIL: THE REAL MONSTERS OF SOCIETY. THE EGO.

I RECEIVE MANY QUESTIONS AND INQUIRIES about all sorts of things from dating and relationship advice to what happens when we die. In the following chapters in this book are some of the things that my Spirit team of Guides and Angels has shared with me in my life. This particular chapter contains words that my spearheading guide, Saint Nathaniel, has relayed to me with his team of disciples who reside in another dimension in the spirit world. He has played an integral part in contributing the tough love messages I voice that essentially come from God. He is someone who does not mince words as I have previously stated in the introduction of this book. He has even scolded me the way a stern Father might. It is not cruel, but out of love. I have interpreted and worded the message as best I can, even though pronouns may be confusing at times. You should still be able to grasp the concept and the ultimate message.

Saint Nathaniel's message
interpreted by the author:

Prejudices towards other people who are different from you have been going on for centuries. Someone's skin color is a different shade, or their features appear much different than yours, or they have a different religion or sexual orientation than you or your community and they are lambasted, criticized, attacked and at times killed! You would think that after all these years on Earth and the progression of civilization that you would have learned something while you have been here. Instead you allow other people and their surroundings to easily influence you causing one to form a false reality. You were all placed here to teach, learn, experience and give love. Why has this most easy and wonderfully uplifting task been so magnificently difficult for some of you? You are all here for this reason. Working on those attributes accelerates your soul's growth. You have been given a body as a protective shell to function while on Earth. Your Spirit soul is your true self and who you are at the core. Your body is a vessel you are renting for a short amount of time in order to live and function in the Earth's dense atmosphere. You came into this world for a purpose and it is your goal to find out what that is and master it. It can be something as simple as learning to forgive others or to control your anger. You must discover this purpose on your own.

Your body is not meant to last eternally, but your soul is. Your bodies were designed to age over a period of time. There is no avoiding this. You can have all the plastic surgery you want in an attempt to keep your outer appearance appearing young. This will not stop the process internally. Your health and organs that keep your soul alive in your body will eventually falter, fail or stop working. This is nothing to be afraid of. The sooner you realize this, then the quicker and easier your transition will be into the spirit world or whatever labels you associate Heaven to be for you. The average Earthly existence is a day long in comparison to life in the next world. When you pass on to the next life, your body is left to disintegrate on Earth and is no longer needed as you move on to paradise. This presents many challenges for those in this lifetime. The

Ego has become a wild and unruly monster crippling millions of human souls. You force feed negative images and stories to one another on a daily basis off of the internet alone which you have created. This ranges from salacious gossip sites to antagonistic news sites and sources that only feature the worst press worthy information provided specifically to control your Ego. They blow it up and sensationalize it. The planet and its people are hypnotized succumbing to its allure. They take pieces of this behavior and incorporate it into their personalities. They then impose it onto friends, family and communities who do the same to others. Suddenly you have this wave of negativity and gossip that has taken over the planet. This energy magnetizes it back to one another ten fold causing a flurry of anger and toxicity that plagues your bodies, souls and your surroundings.

You go to the comment boards on the Internet or wherever those who have too much time on their hands frequent and you find criticisms and negative statements about someone else. The destructive tendencies of the human Ego are alive and well. This was not what we intended for your soul. You did not agree to this when you chose to live an Earthly life. You forgot who you are my child. We do not say any of this to punish or judge you. The only judging that takes place is the one you produce. You take everything personally and react negatively mirroring it back to one another. Soon you have a minefield of bickering and snide energy that is unleashed on the Internet and social media alone. This is transported into the heavens and reflected back to all of you tenfold. Some of you do this callously and naively. In this state you are emulating your lower selves. Many of you are not learning from your mistakes, and nor are you aware of how you treat others, while some of you do not care at all. You are lost in a field of ugliness that you perpetuate daily. You feed off of it and on each other's Egos to one up the next person and make sure your opinion is the one that is gold.

There was a story in the news about a brave fourteen-year-old girl activist from Pakistan. She posted a blog about women having the right to an education. She continued on her crusade despite threats from the Taliban. As a result, the Taliban stopped the school bus she was on and shot her in the head and neck leaving her in critical condition. This is the difference between a girl with no choice and one in America who has several choices. The media and their peers are leading the youth of today. They are more interested in attracting sex or looking desirable than fixing this world. Still—they are more spiritually inclined than any of the previous generations. They have been chosen to bring peace and love into this world as long as they do not follow the path of the Ego.

Some religions preach about a Hell and a Devil. The real Hell is on Earth and the Devil resides in all of you and has been unleashed with great magnitude. The impact is greater than the largest tidal wave, earthquake or meteor rock to ever threaten to smash into Earth. Those who stand in front of a pulpit to deliver fiery sermons are not protected or exempt from this. They are given a platform to reach many responsibly and are not encouraged to misuse that position as some do. Young people pose provocatively online. They are naive and heavily influenced by the mirage of the internets fictitious attention. The photos show where their self-esteem is at which is not in a good place to begin with. This is what some of you feel the need to do to receive instant validation, which is not true confirmation at all. They learn this message from their parents, peers, communities and media. It is a vicious cycle of mythology that has no truth. Your beauty shines through regardless of provocative poses. Many of you tend to put up these photos for various reasons. Sometimes it is just for fun and other times it is an attempt to feel validated and loved. This opens up a bigger can of worms and another plethora of issues that need to be addressed in the world by your media.

There is a rush that some of you get from what seems like positive attention. It is not positive attention as it is false devotion. You are not being loved for who you are, but how you look and what you have. The last two are products of the Ego when in truth you were born with God's holy light regardless of your belief systems. You have discovered that when you post hyper-sexualized photos that you receive more attention. No one is paying attention to you or your true soul dear one. You are blinded by what is not real. Nothing you can do can take away God's love for you. These are good children who are misguided. It prompts them to get love through unhealthy sources that only lower your self-esteem. It makes us sad to see people agonize and suffer for attention that is all a hallucination to begin with. Who you are in spirit and what you set out to do is who you truly are. How you treat others and the love and compassion that you display for others is why you are here. Stay away from gossip, negativity, hate or institutions that persecute others. You are all to be a role model of peace and love allowing God's light to shine within and around you.

When you pass on to the other side, your bodies are left behind and your soul is in tact and healthy in all ways again. What we in spirit see is a glow around us and around you. This glow has a varying brightness depending on one's spiritual evolvement and growth on Earth. On the other side, it is your glow that is looked upon with the love and attraction you crave. On Earth you are attracted to the physical look of the body your soul was born into. This attraction is removed as the body ages and dies. Your soul then becomes a light and that light is the main attraction to other souls. If you are inclined to be an attractive soul, then focus inward and work on your spiritual growth and become who you truly are and always have been. Look within and ignore the rest of it around you.

A dark fog layer has been created around the Earth's atmosphere. This is due to things like the high amount of toxins that human souls consume into their bodies feeding their emotional states and with the venom they emit at each other. This is a layer of thick smog particles that appears as heavy tar. It separates the Earth plane from the Spirit plane. It cannot be seen by the naked eye. If you are in a big city such as Los Angeles you can see the brown dirt that envelopes it looking like a dirty run down mess. This is smog and no one pays any mind to it. They freely breathe in those deadly particles every second and strangely do it without concern. You cannot see it unless you climb up to the top of the Hollywood Hills and look down on it or you are on an airplane landing at Los Angeles Airport. This tar is far worse than that as it is made up of dangerous energy. You are all made up of energy. When someone gets angry around you, then everyone in that vicinity soaks that up ruining everyone else's day. It can incite unnecessary anger or sadness out of them. People are not accustomed to function on top of one another, as

the energy is too intense and not conducive on Earth. People are having
Children that they should not be having. They make many excuses such
as God has asked them to multiply. This was not what God intended.
Man has taken it upon himself to decide what he expects are best for him
and his surroundings allowing his Ego to dictate. This includes those
that pick and choose from your holy books on what you want to believe
in and follow. Most of the time they pick and choose the content that
they believe gives them an excuse to cause destruction, wars, pollution
or any other manipulative energy and harm. They use it as an excuse
to suppress others and as a reason to justify their criticisms as if they are
high and mighty and the rest have no business with life. This was not
what God intended. He is wondering why all of the content on love and
compassion—the most important parts of your holy books have been
ignored. Those that do not have babies for the sake of multiplying have
had them out of ignorance, in poverty or to satisfy the Ego such as the
hole and void within you. Others have children to save their marriage,
relationships or to prevent their partner from leaving them. The only
ones that suffer the most are the children followed by society.

There are some non-believers of God who contribute to the mass
hysteria by allowing their Ego to give them free license to function as
an animal might. They are irresponsible towards themselves and others
by behaving without consequence. Who are you more likely to believe?
Someone headed towards a path of love or hate? Those who choose not
to believe do so in order to have an excuse to treat others or themselves
unkindly. Now Earth is overloaded and crowded with toxins that are
magnified beyond your comprehension. You are in a critical state that
needs immediate attention and change within all of you. It is up to you
as an individual soul. No one else can or will do it for you.

There are those that have been called out into the open to usher
people down the path of the Spirit. They are here to improve this world
and fill it with the love and peace that God intended it to be. They
are around you now or are souls prepping to be born into new human
bodies for Earth's future. They are easy to recognize as some of them
are ushering in peace while others are spreading love. They are working
to clean up the environment and the surroundings on Earth. Some of

them are teaching tolerance and love. You can easily recognize them as they have purposes that all lead to the same target: love, peace or joy. You feel a euphoric happiness of joy when you are in love, experiencing love or giving love. You do not feel this when someone is seeking to harm, hurt or hate. These are the three "H's". You label each other with derogatory words. Most of them come from those that are rigid in their Earthly beliefs and who are blocked from love. These are construed as values when it comes to your political beliefs. This is a waste of time as what is destined to happen is already set. Inciting anger and hostility towards others will not sway it. Some will be happy with the outcome while others will be forced to adapt or fall more into anger and hostility. In the end no one wins. The Devil sees you as disposable as he is what you have become. Your lack of love and help for your fellow man or your fellow brother has humiliated yourself. I am God. You are to love with all the compassion in your heart that I have given you from the moment your soul came to be.

One of your greatest challenges is that God gave you all Egos. There is no way to run from what might feel like a prison, but in essence is instilled to help you grow. Even the nicest most spiritual being has an Ego. This was God's plan since you are all here to learn lessons. You cannot learn specific lessons if everything is made easy for you. The decisions you make everyday make up your character. Your Ego tests you as the Devil would since they are one in the same.

Here's a scenario: You are broke and living check to check, but one day you find that your bank made an error and deposited $75,000 into your account. Do you notify the bank of the error or do you assume it was for you to spend it and you do? This is where someone's Ego can get in the way. It's where most of you were taught the differences between right and wrong. Be kind and accepting of your neighbor. How many of you are living like this? How many of you are teaching your kids this? In the example of the bank error, your decisions will eventually catch up with you and so will the bank and your authorities. Now you have committed an Earthly crime. You had not done anything like that before. This split decision happened when your Ego jumped in the way and dictated a false move on your part.

Because you are all born with Egos it is God's will for you to rein it in and keep it under control. The most spiritually evolved uses the least amount of Ego. Where you hear judgment from others, then this is the Ego at its worst. The Ego is the reason you have witnessed the destruction of God's planet. You were meant to take care of his gift and not destroy it. It is the reason there is abuse, violence, wars, anger, murders, ugliness and negativity. You have had centuries to improve and yet although progress has been made, boy, are you slow! It should not have taken you thousands of years to get nowhere. Why have so many human souls not caught up with the program? The energy of the world is a loaded gun and a ticking time bomb.

There are angels that alternate surrounding the Earth with angel wings covering the entire atmosphere to keep the energy contained 24/7. Earth is the most volatile, violent and hostile planet in the galaxy where everyone is firing harsh energy bullets at once. The Earth's atmosphere is like a pressure cooker that can destroy the entire planet. The energy emanating off the angels wings looks like stardust particles in a massive meteor shower. Only the sensitive, intuitive are able to sense it or even see it. They are the ones that are on Earth saving you from emanating destruction. The others including the abuse of power and yes even the self-righteous that are delusional in thinking they are good are contributing to the damage. This includes those hiding behind false collars preaching erroneous, harmful information. Those that fall into Ego and attack back are no different. Peaceful interaction or no interaction at all from both sides is insisted upon in Heaven.

I am one in millions who serve humanity and Heaven to contribute to the improvement of a place to prevent it from rapidly dying. We gave you things like the Internet and cell phones to be able to connect and communicate positively with one another and look what you have done with it. It has grown to be devices for narcissism and cruelty. Thank God there are those who use it for good. The media and gossip channels are the worst offenders using the devices to lure in the most fragile who succumb to operating from the lower self full time. There is something we find eerie about strangers pasting their thoughts about what other people are doing which is perversely sick. This does nothing to improve your soul.

You have made Hell on Earth and it is what man creates for himself and others like him. The sooner everybody accepts this truth the quicker there will be peace on Earth. It is time for those who are on the receiving end of this nonsense to put their foot down and say, "I am not going to take responsibility for you, because you are not doing your job. Your heart is closed. I will no longer be punished because of your indifference. I will not take responsibility because you have chosen to be unhappy and are thrusting that upon others." After centuries of evolution not only have you forgot how to love and spread joy to others, especially strangers, you have been stuck praying and hoping that one man, a President or ruler, will pull you out of your difficult and struggling lives. The difficulty and struggle you experience is your Ego. Religion and Politics are two belief systems you have created through Free Will that cause wars, anger and hostility towards other human souls. Two belief systems that become completely obsolete and irrelevant the second your soul leaves your body. You are in the midst of grand chaos and it is time to wake up and snap out of it. It is more efficient and effective to have compassion and accept everybody's differences rather than trying to force them to change. There is peace and harmony that way and you accomplish more.

Everyone is struggling and suffering and they believe that someone in your government can fix that. It does not matter who is running things. You have all had the same issue decade after decade. After September 11, 2001 you saw the economy collapse as you went to war, then jobs were lost and businesses closed. Many of you lost a lot of money. Human souls passed away into the next life over the stress of being unable to find a job or the loss of their homes and families. You are arguing over triviality, over who should be allowed to marry who, and who should be killed and hurt. Where is the love? What happened to helping those in need? What happened to healing your neighbor and saying one kind word to someone else? Why are you not mobilizing to improve those living in poverty, the children or your economy and way of life? Why have you allowed your concerns to be misguided?

Politics, religion, bullies and your gossip media are the biggest and loudest Ego offenders in the world causing the most damage to the Earth.

The damage that is done to other people is because they are operating from their lower selves. If everyone operated from there higher selves there would be peace on Earth. Everyone would be experiencing joy and love. We in Heaven see your flawlessness and your inner light. We know your most intimate intentions, thoughts and feelings. You can never get away with a lie in Heaven the way you can with each other on Earth. If on the outside you put on the act with someone to manipulate and get what you want from them, Heaven knows your true intentions and will block you in the end. You may briefly obtain what you wanted out of manipulation, but ultimately it will backfire, as we do not have your back if you have intention to harm, hurt or hate. We will never truly abandon you as we see the love deep inside you and will continue to guide you down the right path. We do not condone evil or assist those that seek to inflict pain or hurt on someone else. We want to work with each of you to improve God's Earthly paradise.

You are here to learn lessons and some of you have to go through it the harder way as you are newly here as a soul. Others have reincarnated repeatedly to gain spiritual wisdom while the rest have come into this life to help change and fix God's world. If you are cut off from spiritual wisdom and in being good to your neighbor and instead opt to do bad things, then you will have to repeat and repay that Karmic debt.

Crises mode was hit as you entered into the year 2000's. Your economy started to tank, jobs were lost, companies were closing up and then an abundant amount of your homes fell into financial ruin. This did not happen immediately so the average human soul might not have noticed. It happened in trickles until the energy around the globe grew to be particularly nasty. Adding to that, you have more people living on Earth than ever before. This magnetizes the energy that is put out there if you are operating from your Ego. You are granted Free Will to set up life as you see fit. Around the mid-1940's having babies and lots of them became the thing that human souls decided was best to do. You call this the Baby Boom or the Baby Boomer age, which reportedly ran until the mid-1960's, but it actually continued into the 70's and 80's as well. It was what was expected of you by each other. You would grow up, become an adult, then immediately get married and start a family.

You were programmed Stepford Wives. Looking back on history, you can see how and where you have been conditioned and programmed as a whole.

The world is now the most crowded it has ever been and people are suffering in all ways because of this. With the decline in available jobs many people around the world have been out of work. You have a rise in population and a decrease in available jobs. You have a rise in the cost of living for an apartment or house while minimum wage and the average job pay stays relatively the same. This is one of many imbalances in your lives. The population will gradually decline over the years, as the newer generations of human souls are thankfully not looking to get married and start having babies. They are thinking for themselves as opposed to the bulk of previous generations. They are being born into new parents in order to stop this madness you have created. You may not notice this shift immediately. By the time the shift is noticeable it will take about another hundred years. It will be a more peaceful and accepting world then. We are moving out of your final Dark Age. Earth will one day be a place of massive joy that the upcoming generations are being born to will make happen. You are evolving, finding joy and are teaching it to many of your kids and so forth now. It is a gorgeous mighty movement uprising in the midst of this negative energy from others. You all are each other's brothers and sisters. Encourage everybody to act and behave responsibly with yourselves and with those around you. This includes not having children you cannot afford or never wanted. You put it in your minds that you are under the impression that this is what God intended. He intends for you to love and to give love to everyone around you. Bring forth children only out of love and out of loving households and relationships.

It can be taxing to you soaking up all that nonsense energy out there in the world child. Walk away from those that express coldness or hostility towards you. You were meant to melt all of their icy hearts. Coldness in someone is a learned trait from when you were children. Coldness in someone is due to someone who does not or has not received much love or is ignored. This started with ones parents or society being aloof and dismissive towards that person during their critical developmental years.

Coldness is not to be confused with introversion which is a shy social veneer that might make one seem cold, but is not once you delve deeper. Cold people lack love in their life and therefore need your assistance more than ever to see the light and joy around them.

One of your quests on learning to love is that you are tested repeatedly by those that may not be walking the talk or who are not spiritual, but superficial. While you are working on your life purpose and contributing to humanity and your surroundings in a positive way, you may wonder what they are offering besides annoyance and grief. God, Heaven and the Angels see the love and true self in every one of you including the worst parts of you. Your criticisms and judgments are wasted words and energy. You have to share this world with those that may operate purely from the lower self. Some of those people are to have an Earth life and will likely reincarnate and have to go through it again if they do not learn something or grow on the first round. You are all evolving at different stages in your lives. Circumstances that might seem as if they are happening to you are actually happening for you in order for you to change and grow. This is a form of evolving. Otherwise you spend your whole life staying at the same level and not learning anything—which for some souls will do just that. They are unaware of the need to learn from the challenges and signs that life is giving them and therefore repeat the same patterns throughout this lifetime staying exactly where they are.

The generations have changed throughout the previous Dark ages. More and more parents today have come into this world at this time in order to incorporate these methods and spiritual principles when raising their children so that you will be that much closer to world peace and having harmonious and joyful lives. This is a far cry from the more rigid fear based ways of the past where certain customs had to be upheld and were passed on from generation to generation. New crops of warriors of god's light are being born into this world to usher in this brighter shift of human souls by teaching about love and passing it down the family lines. It is a mighty movement that is being created. Those that are not on board are gradually dissolving out of the way.

FROM THE AUTHOR

The angry, negative or bitter way of living does not work anymore and nor does a lynch mob society. It's all just noise whenever people's Ego and values are bruised. People want freedom to say and speak whatever they choose only if it jives with their morals. It's the Ego and lower self that is screaming to be noticed and heard. When you experience worry, fear or unease over anything you are giving it energy and attention, both of which expand into more of the same. You do not want to conjure up a self-fulfilling prophecy and cause negative circumstances to hit you.

Do you ever notice that when something goes wrong, that it is followed by more of the same? You may often say, "Why does everything keep happening to me?" It's because you are planting heavy focus on it. Sometimes it's difficult at first to not feel distress over a negative issue, but it is important to take a step back and detach from it. The Ego can be powerful if you allow it to. It gets a rush out of controlling you and creating apprehension or fear about things that are not based in reality. There is one way you can tell the difference between heavenly guidance and your lower self or Ego. When you receive messages from heavenly spirits, you will never experience fear, anxiety or dread. The messages they relay are full of love, even if they are warning you of something negative. There is still a sense of peace or an uplifting feeling that all is okay.

Chapter Three

WHAT HAPPENS TO OUR SPIRIT
AND SOUL WHEN WE DIE?

THERE ARE VARYING THEORIES AND beliefs as to what happens when we die. I will explain what my Spirit team has shared with me over the years. They say there is no pain when you die. If there was a car wreck or someone was shot, your soul is pulled out of your body before that happens. Some of you worry that your loved one suffered death horribly with a gunshot or car wreck for example. My Guides and Angels have shared with me that there is nothing to fear or worry about as there soul exited the body beforehand. Our souls are designed that way. It is still possible for the body to be moving or jolting moments after the soul has left the body. It appears as if they are still alive, but they are not. They are alive in the sense that your soul does not die, but lives on. However, the body is no longer being used. When your soul exits your body you may even hear a sound or a pressure change when it happens. When we pass on, our spirit and soul goes into what appears to be a large tube or a gigantic tunnel that leads to a Light. I found this process into the different soul planes ironically similar to our own human birth that we are accustomed to knowing. The tunnel is nothing to be afraid of and in fact they have told me you will have never felt this incredible. You realize that all the burdens of the body and the physical world had previously felt like one huge painful weight beforehand. You grow to become ecstatically happy and feeling the enormous joy you were born with. What you are doing and where you are heading as you travel to the other side feels perfectly natural to you.

The Light up ahead at the end of the tunnel grows brighter as you approach it. You are moving towards a paradise as one might have imagined it in their dreams of how Heaven or the Other Side to be. It is ten times more stunning than in your dreams. Depending who you believed in while living in your Earthly body, whether it be Buddha or Moses, that would be who would be in the mix of souls to greet you. If you were a Jesus follower, then you would immediately meet Jesus who welcomes you with open arms. If you were an atheist and you head towards the light you will be greeted by angels, your guides and past relatives and family from centuries back embracing you with a big party. There is no judgment before God, but there is what is referred to as a life review. You go through a process where the bad things you have done are replayed for you. The reason is so that you own up to what you have done if you had not made amends during your Earthly life. This is not a form of torture and you are not being judged. The only judgment that is happening is your own as you feel, sense and know the brevity of how you behaved and towards whom. If you caused harm or hurt to someone, then that would be made known to you. Yes, even your ex-lovers will know what you went through when they hurt you. They will feel what you had felt with great veracity. The pain someone else felt that you caused is felt by you in a much stronger way than you would feel it as a human soul. Part of the reason for this is that as a human soul you have attributes of denial and indifference. This is shed as you exit the body.

When you were in your body and in the Earth's intense atmosphere you had a larger Ego than you do as you enter the spirit world. You have a much clearer mind and you are aware and affected by damage you had done to others on Earth. You know, see, feel and hear what you have done with great impact. You proceed from that point when you experience remorse and own up to your mistakes. This is part of your spiritual growth to move on to the next step. You have to make amends for what you have done or how you have caused pain to others. You will feel both how you felt as well as how the other person did in result of your actions. When you reach a place of forgiveness for yourself and others, then you move onto the next stage. You are shown the good things you have done and the impact that created as well. This is why it is important to examine your life now. Look at how you made it from point A to point B. You are going to have to do it when you cross over, you may as well get a head start. You do not have to publish a book, but you can write a timeline for yourself in a journal. I had at first wondered if people wanted to display their life story, but we do it anyway on social networking, reality TV and gossip sites, don't we?

There are different spiritual stages on the spiritual plane so you will not necessarily be in the same stage as other people are. This is the same as it is on Earth where everyone is at a different spiritual stage. We see this in all the religions that exist such as Christian, Hinduism, Muslim and Jewish etc. The only difference is everyone on Earth is in varying spiritual stages all together whereas in the spiritual plane you are around those who are in similar stages of development. If you were walking the path of love you won't be around someone like Adolf Hitler who has had to go through his own life review sessions when he crossed over. His sessions had gone on indefinitely as he was made to feel and experience the pain he caused in others just as we will do. Because he destroyed so many human souls, he is walked through each and every one of those souls feeling and experiencing what they went through. This is a lot of people he has had to go through and make amends with.

Hitler also took his own life, which has its own repercussions. When you take your own life, you are doing this before your time. There are several things that happen. Many who take their own lives have to go through another kind of spiritual training to get them to a place where they can assist those on Earth who are suicidal. There are some who may opt to go back to Earth and incarnate again for another run or class

37

while others are asked to go back. If you exit before your time then you will have to repeat it. Some of us are on Earth to have an Earthly existence, where others such as myself, were given an accelerated crash course of several lifetimes rolled into one for a purpose. They don't tell you what your mission or purpose is because you may rush to complete it before your time. Since I am someone who wants to get the job done immediately, they know I would no doubt get started right away. It is up to you to come to that realization on your own time.

When our souls exit our bodies, we are ushered into the Light, but you are not forced into the Light. If you as a departing Spirit are afraid of the Light due to fears of being told of Hell, damnation and judgment when living, then you may choose to avoid the Light. Atheists may avoid the Light or not truly understand what has happened to them. They might choose to stay in the Earth's spirit atmosphere, which is no place for any departed soul. That spirit stays stuck in what some might call purgatory or limbo mode roaming the Earth and attaching themselves to human souls. If the spirit was a drug addict or alcoholic they will glob onto a human soul who is on Earth abusing or using those vices. They make it worse for that human soul by doing this as they coax that person on to continue drinking, doing drugs or any other harmful habit. These are the same spirits where people have reported Hauntings or a negative presence. If you are experiencing a haunting or a negative spirit, call on God and the Archangel Michael and his band of mercy angels to take that soul into the Light. They can do so on your behalf even if the soul had previously chosen to avoid the Light. We have the power to request their removal on our behalf. I equate it to making a 'citizen's arrest', except they are not going to a place that is similar to jail, but going to a place they will later wish they had done so to begin with. Many atheists immediately discover there is life after death and they love how they feel when they cross over that they do not doubt going into the Light as the process is happening. Choosing atheism is a learned trait and a decision based on Free Will choice just as any other Earthly belief system.

The Light is nothing to fear, as it is all love where your wildest dreams can be conquered and felt. You can build that dream home you always wanted. You do not need money to buy it. Your Earthly burdens such as jobs and health worries are no more. You are who you were before you agreed to be born into an Earthly body. You experience God's love in ways you wish you had allowed yourself to be part of all of this Earthly life. All the solutions you had wondered about while on Earth are answered. You come to the realization that it was all about pure love. You weep with tears of joy to know and understand that love in ways you had always wished you had. You discover that all of the things you took for granted were things as simple as the trees, flowers, the oceans, nature's wonders and above all love. You see how man is destroying the habitat and you wish you had done something to contribute to its survival. You can choose any route you like whether that is to train as a Spirit Guide, prepare the new souls that are arriving, or even reincarnate and have another Earthly life at a later time. There are many different paths and choices you can make with your team on the other side. You may choose to reincarnate at just the right time in history to contribute something that will continue to improve the Earthly life. Earth life progresses slower than any other habitat. We are the slowest to learn and grow as a whole. When you cross over it is your inner light that is attractive and not your exterior looks. The brighter your light is, the hotter you are!

Many grieved in the year 2012 when a man shot his Mother multiple times and then went to a Connecticut Elementary School with a high-powered rifle to shoot many children, some adults and then himself. It was added to history as a perfect example of true evil that exists in human beings. The children's souls that crossed over were extricated from their bodies before the bullets hit. The day this happened when many were grieving and upset, I was shown that the children were doing great and were in recovery. This is not the recovery we think of after a surgery. It looks to me like peaceful comforting and healing hyper-sleep. The souls were fine and surrounded by God's Light. Many angels nursed their souls to full potential. When the souls woke up they felt immeasurable love and joy. They feel no pain or grief during this process, but the departed souls are concerned when they see there loved ones on Earth upset. The children's souls soon visited with their grieving families not long afterwards. Days after the deaths, my guides had shown the children to me at one of the most stunning gorgeous playgrounds one has seen in Heaven. They were surrounded by Mother Mary, Jesus and Archangel Gabriel—all of who are so powerful and unlimited they can be with anyone who asks. I found it interesting that they were the three that came through, because according to some religious beliefs, it was Archangel Gabriel who announced the coming of the birth of Christ and the new age of Pisces. Here Archangel Gabriel was with Jesus and Mother Mary surrounding the children's souls with their light after their passing.

Some have asked that if there is a God then how can He have allowed this shooting to happen. We are granted Free Will choice. This is in order for us to learn the difference between right and wrong as well as for our spiritual growth. The shooter's mind was wrecked with anger and pain from being bullied at the school beforehand. The shooter's guardian spirits did attempt to help and stop him, but if you are not listening or paying attention to the communication that your Guides and Angels are making, then little can be done at that point. His mind had blocked out the Divine communication that was coming in with the wasted feelings of anger and pain. I was told that they did warn him as well as the mother repeatedly for some time, but both ignored the messages coming from Heaven as so many human souls do. This is why it is crucial for all of us to have a clear mind and live a healthy life so that we can pay attention to the Divine messages that are given to us to make our lives easier. This is also why if we listened to our own Guides and Angels we would have peace on Earth.

When we cross over our families from many of our previous lives, as well as our Guardian Angel and Spirit Guide greet us in the spiritual plane. We meet our Spirit team and the ones we were communing with all through our life on Earth. You will know immediately that you are truly home showered with God's impenetrable Light of love. You will know who the people are who greet you in the Spirit world even if you did not know of them while on Earth. Your memory of who you once were as a soul before entering a human body grows to be fully in tact. We meet our Twin Flame if they are on the other side waiting for us.

People often ask me if they can have sex or eat when they cross over. The answer is yes. All of our senses are awakened when we cross over and we are in peak form.

If one wants to partake in certain pleasures they enjoyed on Earth they most certainly can. What they do tell me is there is a difference between that and someone who is obsessed by carnal desires. Satisfying carnal desires stops your spiritual growth because you are feeding the Ego and/or emptiness within you. This is not to be confused with having a healthy sexual appetite that is kept under control. If you are reuniting with your soul mate or twin flame on the other side and you both had an active sex life or love together on Earth and want one in the spiritual realm, you may choose to continue. Only this time it is better than any other sex you have ever had because all of your senses are heightened to a great degree. You are not burdened with the physical problems that plague our human bodies and psyches such as daily stress, depression or impotence. If you have those issues while on Earth, they are lifted and left with your body when your soul leaves its human vessel.

I have had people ask me if the spirit world watches us have sex on Earth. The answer is no. They see us all as varying lights and have no interest in spying on you during fornication, unless it is harmful to your Spirit in some way. They are around to guide us down the right path and steer us away from danger or mistakes. They know your thoughts and feelings as well as what is to come for you in your life next if you continue on the path you are on. There are things we need to learn first before we reach a place of knowing our mission. For some people they may have known immediately what their mission was as a child, but might not have known how it would apply to them until later in life.

When you cross over you will be brought to peak form. This means any health issues you were having are no more. If your human body had gained tons of weight you slim right back down. If you used a wheelchair you would not need it when you cross over. Any deterioration you might have had happened to your body is rejuvenated. Although you can appear however you choose which includes the image and age you were when passing on, you do typically appear what would seem around ages 27-34 in human years. If a loved one on Earth has heightened clairvoyance able to see Spirits on the other side, you may not be entirely recognizable to them immediately. The reason is if you were overweight at that age or had a different look, you do not exude that look. It will look like you, but slightly different and more beautifully profound and strong.

We are souls temporarily inhabiting the bodies that we came into this Earth life with and then the body will be of no more use. The body is allowing us life on Earth to learn how to love and experience life lessons so that our soul can grow and be ready for the next plateau. In order to be on Earth our soul has to inhabit a physical body. The body is formed within a female human being whom we chose to enter this life from. Even if the woman gives their child up for adoption, you still chose that particular person to enter this life from knowing that she would not raise you. If we live a long life, then the bodies we use will grow old as an indicator that your life run has been complete. Actual Earth age years have no relevance to anything beyond that. This certainly contradicts the Media and society's ageism discrimination that they have created and taught the public. This is a product designed by the Ego and is not based in reality.

There was a night where I jolted awake to the smell of an exotic flavored sandwich. It was so potent as if someone was cooking it in my bed. It was a spirit from the other side hanging around me. When this spirit lived an Earthly life in the early 1900's, he loved ordering these sandwiches everyday at his local deli for lunch. My light is so bright that these spirits are drawn to it. The light grows even brighter at night due to the fact that I am in a more relaxed state and away from the stress of the constantly busy streets. I naturally inquired as to why he was eating when I was under the impression that you don't need food on the other side. One of my guides said, "Your soul does not require food here. You are able to manifest the things you want or once loved when you were living on Earth." This is true pending it is not harmful to your soul. In this case, this spirit wanted to continue eating those sandwiches he so enjoyed when living an Earthly life. Of course the sandwich is ten times better than the deli made it where he is now. The windows were closed and it was in the middle of the night. There was no one cooking and even if they were those smells never reach my room.

ABORTION

I have been asked about Heaven's views on abortion. There are souls in Heaven who want to have an Earthly life for the purposes of growth, learning or for a specific purpose that will benefit humanity in a positive way. Those souls choose the people that will become their parents beforehand. I naturally had a difficult time accepting that I chose my parents, but it was for the objective of immediate soul growth. Sometimes before the souls have come into an Earthly life, they may play a hand at getting the two specific people to come together in love and marriage or at least to consummate so that they can be born into an Earthly life. They know beforehand which way it is going to go. This same case applies to a woman who chooses to have a baby or wants one. If that woman goes to a sperm donor, the same process applies where that soul is choosing to be brought up by that mother. If the mother is a surrogate, the soul is fully aware that they will enter this life through that mother, but someone else will be their parent. They will know who that is as well, but will not have memory of this once born. If a woman decides that she wants, chooses or needs to have an abortion, then she is essentially preventing the soul from having an Earthly life. When someone responded to my statement, "So then you're pro-life?" I am not either. I do not make the choices for an individual and nor do I pass any judgment on either side. I merely relay what I am told and you take and do what you will with it.

The mother that is having this abortion is not technically killing the child as the soul experiences no pain. For the soul, it is more like, "Okay, back to the drawing board." The mother that is making the Free Will choice to have the abortion is in a sense preventing that soul from having a chosen Earth life. However, the soul that is aborted will have priority dibs on choosing another set of parents to enter this life with or they can choose to stay in the Spirit world and perform other functions and duties.

If a woman has a miscarriage then the same scenario still applies as well as if it were an abortion. If the mother who had a miscarriage or aborted a previous pregnancy is pregnant again, then that same soul is allowed to be first in line to re-enter the Earthly plane through that chosen mother. For those that have miscarried and eventually had a baby this can be comforting news to know that it is likely the same soul from before. The soul may choose not to re-enter, but may choose to be the Spirit Guide or Guardian Angel of the next child the mother has. Or they may assist the mother with not miscarrying at a later date. Exercise safe sex practices and be responsible when creating a baby.

Chapter Four

RAISING YOUR VIBRATION
TO A HIGHER LEVEL

IN THE NEXT TWO CHAPTERS my Spirit team has asked that we look at fine-tuning that Divine communication instrument that is your body and soul. We are all aiming for the same goal in this life. We want to be consistently happy more than anything in the world. We want to accomplish and have our dreams come true. When we live our daily lives unhappy with the way things are, we reach for an *addiction* or a *time waster*. It is peculiar that we feed our bodies and our soul garbage. What is the point of living if you're not enjoying the moment focused and clear? We'll justify or make excuses for our bad behavior. We'll tell others I'm not going to be made to feel guilty. I'm just going to do it this one time and yet you end up doing it more than just once. Before you know it six months have passed and it has become a regular habit again. When you look back on those past six months you discover you haven't accomplished anything. You are exactly where you were before and still negative and despondent.

The reason it is important to fine-tune your body and soul is that you open up the portal to receive Heavenly communication and assistance. You have more energy during the day to accomplish what you want. You look and feel incredible that you attract in wonderful circumstances, jobs, friendships and relationships of a higher caliber. You are happier and more optimistic. This positive energy enhancement shoots outwardly into the universe brightening up its atmosphere. It is hypnotizing and magnetic to others while becoming a recipe for tremendous situations to enter your life. When people are living joyful, happy lives they are more tolerant, accepting and loving to be around. People are not drawn to miserable drunks with a pessimistic attitude problem. When you take care of your body and treat your soul with the utmost respect, then the universe and Heaven returns that back to you tenfold. It raises your vibration closer to God who has all of the answers you are seeking to navigate through what might feel like a rocky life. Your life does not have to be treacherous because you can experience tranquility now. Only when you have reached that place of peaceful contentment do you witness the gifts and miracles you seek.

When you grow and evolve you are raising your vibration. Raising your vibration to a higher level takes work and discipline. It is adopting an entirely new way of living and viewing life, your surroundings and your soul. Some examples of necessary lifestyle changes that will raise your vibration are cleaning up your diet, eating healthier, breathing deeper, avoiding alcohol, drugs and people who are drowning in stress, depression or poor life choices. This is not to say that you should abandon family members or loved ones who are under stress. There is a fine line between getting too involved that you fall into the hole with them and remaining detached. You do not want to get emotionally drawn in. Saying *no* does not mean that you are coldhearted. When you say *no*, you are saying *yes* to you.

Alcohol should be in moderation or eliminated if you have an addictive personality. I understand this being a former addict myself. Even when I was no longer addicted to drugs and alcohol I still went through a period of what is called being a *dry addict* or *dry drunk*. This is someone who is no longer addicted or using drugs and alcohol, but is still behaving as a dysfunctional addict. They have made no positive changes within themselves and therefore are more likely to start going after that initial addiction again.

There are times when it might feel effortless to reach for an alcoholic beverage or more to decompress after a long day. This may relax you for an hour, but then as the effects of the alcohol wear off, you begin to feel lethargic, edgier and even more worn out. You do not realize the array of negative blocks you have created around you. These blocks are dangerous as it prevents the flow of positive energy, light and manifestation to you. It also has adverse health effects to your body and well-being in the long run. It's important to avoid tons of alcohol and other negative vices for escape as much as possible.

Instead of reaching for that drink, I am more inclined to exercise. I jog up a mountain or on the beach. Exercise centers and elevates your spirit. You have more energy in the process while looking and feeling better too! Others notice a brighter glow around you and your entire aura and being attracts others to you. You also have more time in the day to accomplish more important tasks geared towards your life purpose as well as more time for healthy rest. Relaxation is not just a luxury, but it is a necessity. Get away for the weekend and aim for a place somewhere in nature such as a park, the desert, the mountains or the beach where it is quiet and serene. I use those surroundings as an access to re-center myself if I am truly feeling out of sorts. If I'm at home and unable to get away for any reason I'll put on a melodic chill out or classical CD, light some Tibetan incense and candles. I will create a safe, calming sanctuary where I live.

BREATHING AND STRETCHING

Breathing is vital to your health and in raising your vibration. When you are stressed or upset you are holding your breath without realizing it. Take some time daily to sit still, pause and breathe deeply in and out. This is stopping what you are doing, take a huge healthy breathe in, hold it for three to five seconds and exhale out all of your worries, stress and toxins. Imagine the pressures and tension you have bottled and locked up in your body exiting out into the air as you exhale. Do this repeatedly in one sitting and notice how relaxed and clear minded you start to feel. You might experience some lightheadness as you re-center and re-align your body. Doing this breathing exercise also sends and feeds oxygen to all of your organs and cells awakening your soul that can often feel trapped in your body. Taking time to breathe is essential to centering yourself, yet many of us do not take the time to do this. We would rather hold our stress in. This is dangerous over time as it leads to health complications by trapping in all of that unnecessary negativity. Centering yourself helps you to feel whole, focused and euphorically happy. It connects your soul and your body helping you become aware of who you are in truth.

After breathing, it's important to incorporate body stretching into your routine as this not only improves your circulation, but relaxes the muscles that can tense up. Sometimes I will lie down on the floor and stretch every part of my body in various ways. You can do this also by laying a towel down next to your bed. If you are able to bring it to your backyard or a park is even better as it is more of a cheering environment. Sometimes we are not aware that the wear and tear of our day can easily tighten up areas in our bodies. All of the stresses compounded in your day become trapped into the crevices of the cells in your body. Breathing exercises get a lot of that gunk out, but sometimes there are remains of it wedged into hard to reach areas that can later cause health issues. This blocks the flow of good energy and vibrations throughout your body and soul. This is why stretching is beneficial to your overall well-being. I will often talk to certain friends who are bubbly, upbeat or positive as well. Suddenly everything shifts in and around my world feeling those good vibes from optimistic people, stretching and breathing.

CUDDLING, HUGGING & TOUCHING

If you are involved with someone in a romantic relationship, then make love or love each other up constantly. Make regular efforts to shower one another with supportive words. Those that are in long-term, committed, love relationships are physically healthier and happier. They are more productive and live longer than those who are not. There are powerful healing benefits for a couple that are happy and loyal to one another. When you are in a relationship you need to hug one another often, cuddle, make love, kiss and give each other massages after long stress filled days. Do this with one another constantly no matter how ridiculous that might seem to you. If you shun or shy away from this type of physical expression, then you need to let your guard down and open your heart up to your significant other. This is important for your long term health.

Partaking in these activities with your partner lowers both of your cortisol levels and blood pressure. You are less stressful after a day full of too much negative energy. Cortisol is a stress hormone in your adrenal glands above your kidney's that shoots out to your brain when a sudden panic or attack in your life happens. It's not healthy for your brain when it reaches high levels and can be dangerous if there's too much of it. When your nervous system is shot that high too quickly it's not that easy for it to come back down either. For some it can take as long as a day! Most of us have experienced something alarming in our lives at one time or another. You are also likely aware with how long you carried that alarm state in you. That's what this cortisol hormone is. Cuddling, hugging and touching have immense healing properties that it is able to bring down your cortisol levels more rapidly than anything else.

Hold hands and touch your partner often. Touching relaxes you lowering your blood pressure. When you touch your partner it merges your souls. There is the emotional impact that reassures you both that you are protected. This elevates both of your vibrations to a place of contentment and satisfaction. Touching has great benefits for the physical and metaphysical heart.

There isn't enough reaching out and expressions of love in this world to begin with. When someone is exuding negative traits and directing them outwardly towards anyone in their way, they are masking unhappiness inside. Grab them and hug them up to melt those wasted toxic feelings that do not help them or anybody around. Can you imagine that instead of war you hugged your enemies? The vibration of this entire planet would rise to a phenomenal degree creating a beautiful, loving place where all people are happy.

EMOTIONAL EATING

Health and diet are crucial areas of focus that need to be adhered to in order to raise your vibration. We were not meant to consume chips and hot dogs or cause harm and destruction to our bodies and emotional well-being. The mantra that says we must do everything in moderation is important, however, eliminating negative substances altogether is even better. Unfortunately, our Egos get in the way convincing us that we need that piece of chocolate cake. The bad foods and drinks that you consume are emotional eating and a result of something bigger going on underneath.

There is always an underlying emptiness or cause going on within you that prompts you to have repeated cravings for something like Pizza or Ice Cream. God, the angels and spirits in Heaven do not say any of this so that you are miserable. It may seem like that when they urge you to clean up your diet and avoid bad foods, soda, alcohol or drugs. On the contrary, by cleaning up your diet you grow to become more focused and happier in the long-term. You experience longer lasting feelings of pleasure and enjoyment rather than feeling blocked and weighed down by regular pieces of cake. You attract in at higher levels and you awaken your spiritual connection to Heaven. You are also more readily able to hear, see, feel and know the messages and guidance that they wish to relay to you that can assist you on your path. If you do not make these changes and modifications, then you are likely to stay in the same place you have been in your life to date.

HARSH ENERGIES

The energies around the world are harsh everyday and that is just the sad reality now. Despite all this, everything is shifting for the better, but with those shifts come many people throwing tantrums over it. This is what you are bearing witness to. Before the harsh energies came at you once in awhile, but now it is out of control and always happening. Do not continue down the path of living in turmoil and displaying agitating energies. It is important to make certain lifestyle changes that include avoiding harsh situations and people as much as possible. Steer yourself away from all drama, as it is all noise, which are energies that you do not want to be a part of. There is no love that exists in that area and it helps no one.

Due to the energy being particularly intense you all need to balance your lives such as your personal and professional life. This can be getting away for the weekend to do nothing. You do not have to go away if you do not have the money or time. You can go to a park and unwind for a bit. What happens when you are alone in nature amidst the trees and flowers? You start to relax and calm down. You certainly do not relax sitting in your car in traffic or trying to cross a busy street with horns honking and people shooting harsh invisible daggers carelessly in the air. There is great emphasis for you to take these retreats. You all need regular stretches of time off and away from it all to balance the energies in your often stress filled lives. It gives you the opportunity to clear your minds of all that debris. You can ask your Spirit team to give you the time and resources to get away and they will get to work on it.

EXERCISE AND FITNESS

The Earth's atmosphere is extremely heavy and compressed. This blocks us and makes it difficult for many to connect to the Spirit world even though God is constantly connecting with each of us everyday. The stuff we put into our bodies contribute to these blocks including things such as cigarettes, alcohol, drugs, violence, anger, revenge and dysfunctional relationships. Negativity and gossip as well as poor diets and lack of exercise are other factors. This is why it is demanded that we take care of our bodies and be mindful of our life choices and habits.

I'm a strong advocate for health and fitness no matter what age someone is. Since I was ten years old, my Guides and Angels have been sharing with me that exercising and taking care of ourselves physically is our #1 obligation to do while here. You have to take care of your bodies! You have to take care of your body, as it is a gift enabling you to function and accomplish your goals and manifestations while you are living here. You have to care about it and yourself.

Heaven considers certain things a sin, although the word sin isn't in their vocabulary, but the meaning is still the same. One of those sins is: Lack of Exercise. You are urged or yet demanded to take care of your body and to take the vessel you are living in with incredible seriousness. There are some who have elected to come into this life where physical exercise may be impossible. Know that when they say exercise and take care of your body, this is to do it in the best possible way that you are able to. Not everyone can run up a mountain, but there are light cardio exercises one can do. There are stretches one can do or lighter forms of exercise movement. There is a difference between whining that you don't feel like it, have other things to do and are too tired or you physically cannot do it.

Before computers, cell phones and even television sets how did we ever get through the day? We spent more time outdoors! The bigger cities were not as busy and congested as they are now. You could go for peaceful walks right in the middle of the largest city. Now we have to search for a nature preserve of some kind or a park unless you live in such a location. Before the days of electricity and light or clocks for that matter, people did not obsess over the distractions that exist today. We would be outdoors and head to bed when the sun went down so that we had a full day with more energy to accomplish many things the next day.

If I am on caffeine, then hearing my own Guides and Angels is difficult. It is as if the sound has been turned down low. The reason is caffeine speeds up your heart and therefore your anxiety levels. Anxiety and stress block heavenly communication. In order to turn up the volume remove negative substances such as coffee, sodas and other heavily caffeinated drinks. Your body is an instrument designed to receive messages from God when you are operating at a higher frequency. You are unable to do that on vices like caffeine, alcohol or cigarettes. Heavy stints of caffeine increase anxiety and hypertension, which can cause long term health problems as well. When I'm doing something that will affect me negatively, my left ear rings loudly at times. This is my Spirit team's way of getting my attention and downloading information to assist me in dissolving my cravings for these more dangerous, addictive, substance behaviors.

Water is also a critical necessity you need to consume lots of. Our bodies are compiled of water. God created tons of water in and all around us for a reason. This was to ensure that we are able to keep our bodies in working condition. One of the ways this is accomplished is by drinking water. This hydrates and fuels all of your organs flushing out all of the toxins you breathe into your body. These pollutants and waste stay in your body causing damage to your kidneys if they are not rinsed out repeatedly with water. When you drink plenty of water you have more energy, a clearer complexion and not to mention you look better too! I have been drinking over eight glasses of water since I was a teenager. I carry a huge missile of water with me every single day and have been since I was seventeen. One of my many secrets is having a disciplined regimen that includes consuming at least eight glasses of water a day. Your water consumption needs to be done indefinitely.

Exercise is significant in maintaining your body, health and soul. You do not need to be a hardcore body builder or world renowned athlete. My Spirit team has explained to me that some body building lifestyles fall surprisingly into the realm of addictions. These are people that pump themselves up daily with chemicals before they spend hours working on their body. Some of them view their bodies with a distorted view not realizing when they are doing too much. The other form of exercise addiction is with those that only work out purely for vanity reasons. I do cardio such as jogging several times a week. I head to the gym to use the weight machines or the free weights at home. I will randomly drop down to do pushups on the floor or even an empty elevator as it takes me to my location. I am always active and keeping my body as healthy as I can. Exercising and being active has always been like oxygen to me. There are days where my energy level is low, but I push myself to get started with some cardio if even for a short bit. About five to ten minutes of jogging and your blood starts pumping through your organs. Exercise fights feelings of anxiety and depression prompting you to be more alert and energetic.

When you go for a jog, start out by walking briskly for about three to five minutes to get your joints lubricated, and then move into your jog. If it's a short jog, then after about another fifteen minutes give yourself an additional five minutes to cool down at the end. You do not want to stop abruptly and sit down, as that is not good on your heart. There are lighter forms of exercise you may find more suitable for your sensibilities and body chemistry such as Yoga or Tai Chi. Do anything besides sitting on the couch all day, in your cars or in an office chair. Get at least fifteen minutes of brisk exercise everyday. Do it several times a day if you are able to. Get moving! I carry my gym bag everywhere for those days where I decide to head to the gym before I head on home after work. If you go straight home before you go to the gym, you might talk yourself out of going. You are comfortable and just want to relax. Stopping at the gym on the way home has many benefits like giving you a break from rush hour traffic!

REMOVING ADDICTIONS AND NEGATIVE SUBSTANCES

It was not easy or immediate when I was brought to a permanent healthier space in my life. As I mentioned in an earlier part of this book and in my previous book, *"Reaching for the Warrior Within"*, I was a compulsive addict. I was addicted to drugs, alcohol, over the counter prescription medication, cigarettes, coffee, sugar and even dysfunctional relationships and people! One by one my Spirit team started dissolving my cravings for those addictions. I did not go through any professional therapy. I accomplished this with the power of my mind and the help of my Spirit team. I was surprised to find that I was happier not using any of those vices.

Coffee blocks and dims the communication waves to Heaven. My Spirit team had told me I didn't need it. Naturally I argued as I do with anyone who is pushing me to do something I disagree with. I was not a big coffee drinker to begin with, but I did have one cup of coffee every morning. The rest of the day I would be drinking that huge missile of water. I fought with the angels on this. There were others who were far more into their coffee than I was and those people were drinking lots of it. Researchers have said that one-cup a day has shown no negative adverse health effects. I always showed up to battle or to debate by having done my research. Every morning I would get up at 7:30am tired, even after sleeping my mandatory minimum eight hours a night. I would head over to my fancy French press to make that perfect cup of coffee. As I was getting ready I'd continuously hear my Spirit team say, "You don't need it." I'd ignore them and grumble. "Yes I do." I'd need concrete proof that I don't need it in order for me to quit.

One day after the nudges persisted, I slammed my hands down and said, "Okay if you don't believe I need coffee and I think I do, then I give you full permission to assist me in reducing my cravings for coffee. That's the only way I see this working. If I'm craving coffee, then there's no stopping me. I'm going to have it, unless you can help me with this then too." They agreed in succession. The next morning I woke up and went into the kitchen. I felt unusually alive. I thought, "Hmm, I'm not craving any coffee this morning. That's odd. I might try and do without it today. Let's test this out."

About a month later, I discovered that I was only having one cup of coffee a few times a week instead of every single morning. Over the course of the months that followed it was one cup of coffee once or twice a week. This moved into once or twice every couple of weeks. This pattern continued until by month six, I was no longer drinking coffee at all! After twenty years of drinking a cup every morning at that moment, I no longer drink coffee or crave it. I also found I had more energy and was less stressed out by not having had that cup of coffee. I have the coffee bag in my house, but the same bag has been sitting there unused for emergencies or guests. I haven't found the need for an emergency and even if I did, I would not beat myself up over it. You take it all one day at a time and do the best you can as you dissolve unhealthy substances gradually and safely. The way they removed coffee was the same way they removed cigarettes, hard drugs and heavy drinking—all gone just like that. No urge. No craving. It was miraculous as the change happened after I made my official request to my Guides and Angels for help with it.

The world spends billions of dollars on coffee daily. Some buy that fancy cup of coffee every day at whatever coffee franchise is on the way to their work. Imagine spending about $3.00-$4.00 a day five days a week. You're spending $80.00 a month on a coffee drink that has no benefit to your health in the long run. Not to mention it only exasperates your stress and anxiety levels. There are parents who pump their kids up with daily caffeinated soda giving them constant injections of caffeine and sugar. I was one of those kids who would revel in the occasional soda. Luckily, my taste for dangerous food and drinks were earlier in my life. Even while doing it, I was aware that this couldn't be good for me in the long run. You only have one body and you have to take care of it. You have to care about it and yourself immediately. Whatever pain or issues you are focusing on are all self induced by yourself, your Ego or those you surround yourself with. You can eliminate it as I did with the assistance of your own team of Guides and Angels. I was able to gradually change my life and I have never felt as great as I feel today. I had more energy and optimism at thirty-five than I did at twenty-five. I also had more stamina and was more fit than I was then. You can do it too!

Now instead of coffee, I juice one whole cucumber in the morning and will at times add a teaspoon of black gelatinized organic Maca powder. Sometimes if I want a real kick I'll juice a clove of garlic with the cucumber and add a splash of Cayenne pepper spice. This healthy alternative gives me just what I need and in better ways than a measly cup of coffee that would only exasperate my stress, anxiety and depression. I would later crash from the coffee, but the cucumber juice keeps on going. My mind is clearer and the messages from Spirit are opened up. Before this change, the messages were dim and faint. Cucumber juice is also great for your complexion and cleans and clears out the toxins from your organs. It's fantastic on your lymphatic system and far less costly than paying for a daily cup of coffee.

My Guides and Angels then nudged me to reduce and eliminate sugar. I would only sprinkle a little bit in coffee, tea or cereal to begin with, yet I wanted to test it out and see if I could do without it. I stopped sprinkling granulated sugar on anything after that and never went back. Instead I use a healthier alternative such as a spice like cinnamon or nutmeg. Coincidentally nutmeg has its own healing properties. It is great as a brain stimulant and relieves stress and depression among other things. Cinnamon is also high in nutrients and lowers cholesterol. Both are a much healthier alternative to sugar, which has zero benefits and is toxic to your body and health in the end. I was surprised by how much I loved the taste of Cinnamon after that. It far exceeds that of granulated sugar. The same goes for salt. I was never a salt fan, but the rare occasions where salt is needed for myself or a friend, I offer Sea Salt or Himalayan Salt which is not damaging to your body the way processed salt is. In fact, it detoxifies and assists in balancing the energies in your body.

When I quit cigarettes at age twenty-five I had a box hidden away in case of an emergency even though that day never came. It is preferred that you throw away whatever it is you're trying to quit. The reason is you have some of that energy hanging around the house. You also won't be tempted if it is not there. I did eventually throw out the cigarettes. I have never had any cravings for cigarettes after the age of twenty-five. I also cannot stand next to someone who is smoking around me.

As a former addict, I can tell you that most of the people using drugs and alcohol are running from something that includes some form of emotional or mental trauma. There are people who use it because they enjoy the way it makes them feel. If they enjoy the way it makes them feel it's because they don't like how they feel when they're not on anything. Why don't you like how you feel without being on anything? The inadequacy inside you is a false reality. Everyone is too busy fixing their outsides so people will find them attractive or like them, but they are not bothering to correct the core problem, which lies inside you. You are more attractive when you exude that from the inside out. Ask your own Guides and Angels to steer you towards a healthier lifestyle. All you have to do is say the words, "Please help me with…." And then pay attention to the signs and messages that they put in your path.

They also assisted me in completely removing my need or hankerings for anti-depressant and anxiety medication. I was on it after a relationship break up in 2007 and ended up staying on it for three years as I discovered it helped me with my social anxiety. I asked my Spirit team to help me find healthy alternatives that are better for my body. I researched and discovered the right vitamins that were deficient in me. This isn't to say that everyone should do this. You should always discuss dissolving your prescribed medication with your Doctor first. I was determined to live as naturally as much as I could and trust that I would be okay. I was on the drug Effexor for several years and after I asked for help they guided me to a reduced anti-depressant in Wellbutrin. They do not abruptly take you off of something, but gradually wane and reduce you off of your addiction. After six months of the Wellbutrin, I took the last tablet and that was that. I agreed with my Spirit team that I would take it day to day and not push myself any further that I didn't think I could do. I haven't had a prescribed anti-depressant medication tablet since.

It is more than just cutting all of these toxic consumptions out, but I personally had to cut many things out of my life as I shifted into becoming a Warrior of Light. This included the biggest culprits and cause of my addictions, certain people. Toxic, negative and abusive people were all out and gone! Those around you contribute to one succumbing to a pill or vice. Your insufficient and uncomfortable feelings that lead you to the drug were not there when you were born. I had joked with a friend once that people are on medication...because of other people! It's others that should be on medication. Don't give them that power. Tell them no, go away and get lost. It was the Archangel Raphael that helped me off anti-depressants without any support from anyone around me as he altered my entire life into something positive. He had me clear the debris and toxins from within my body and those around me first.

CLEAR THE CLUTTER

Simplify your life and eliminate clutter in and around you to get the positive energy out and moving. We accumulate clutter everyday from material things to other people's energies. The angels have shown me that this clutter is similar to a drainpipe in a sink. When hair and gunk gets stuck in those pipes the water doesn't flow freely. This same concept goes for our bodies and our lives. It blocks good things from flowing easily to and from us as well as good energy streaming through our bodies. We often get stuck in a rutted routine and don't realize how stagnant we've become. Educating yourself and becoming a lifelong student of higher learning is one way to raise your vibration. Your diet and what you consume has an effect on your overall well-being and energy level. High vibrational foods are fruits and vegetables. Avoid sugar, alcohol and foods and substances filled with preservatives. Drugs are a definite no, as it has detrimental effects on your health and the relationships around you. It blocks messages from Heaven and opens the portal for negative energies to attach themselves to you permanently.

I have seen many rave about soy products, which does have positive benefits. However, men should avoid soy or reduce it when possible. This may seem impractical considering that the food industries have chosen to infuse some form of soy in their products. Soy increases estrogen levels in men. The nutrition and diet industries have been feeding the health benefits of soy to the public, but the problem is they are not mentioning the repercussions on men specifically. Kids have been raised on soy now and the boys will hit a hormone drop in their mid-thirties instead of the expected mid-forties. Soy suppresses a man's sex drive because of the drop in testosterone along with other side effects.

Besides waking up the next day with a hangover from alcohol or drugs, do you ever notice that it takes a great deal of effort to get yourself and your body back up to standard? It takes longer than a day to get there and some don't even survive the week without consuming another drink or drug. The older you get, the harder it is on your body, which is why many quit altogether. If they don't, then there poor bodies just give out and stop working resulting in death. They exit this life long before their time.

Retreat often and take vacations to decompress the built up stresses you've added onto your soul. A time out is necessary even if you don't have enough time. Make the time! Eliminate people from your life that drain and suck you dry. Abolish those that lead you to do things that are not healthy for your soul and body. Do it now. I've always been a firm believer that having a drink or that bad food in moderation is okay. Moderation means once in a blue moon. The problem is there are many who slip out of that moderation and it ends up becoming a regular habit. We are here to not only fulfill our life purpose and learn lessons, but to enjoy this life and have some fun. This fun does not fall into the category of toxic. You are not asked to stop for anyone's benefit, but your own. Heaven wants you to live at your fullest potential while experiencing euphoric feelings of joy. When you are healthy, exercising regularly and disciplined about what you put into your body, then the fun and enjoyment you experience is beyond cosmic. If a stressful situation hits you, then as a high vibration soul you are able to take on that stress in stride. You are more equipped to letting it roll off you without tampering with your energy field. The stressed situation also evaporated rather quickly than it would if you had not asked your Spirit team to intervene.

Your individual blocks need to be identified through personal self-analysis. You can do this by being as truthful with yourself as possible so that you can extricate those blocks out of your life immediately. You need to be completely objective during this process and get your Ego out of the way. Blocks are what prevent you from achieving happiness and your wildest dreams of abundance from Heaven.

AVOID GOSSIP

I don't watch regular television and nor do I have it hooked up. I stay away from the news because it's mostly always spun in a negative way to get everyone riled up or to bring them down. It also prompts others to gossip and argue their beliefs and opinions back and forth. This does nothing to help them, the other person or the situation they are arguing about. Yet, it is impossible to not notice the headlines at times when you are checking your email for example. When you read the negative headlines or absorb that energy, then you have invited it into your vicinity to hang out. It tampers with your well-being and your own positive energy. Your self-esteem plummets and your aura becomes dark and muddy. You don't realize it until you are deep in it, then you find you can't easily climb back out of it.

Work on reversing those negative effects that have been built up by being considerate and thoughtful with your media choices. Be mindful of how you communicate with others and who you allow into your world. When you express kindness towards someone else your energy lifts not only yourself, but the other person as well. You are no longer burdened by the weight of that darkness. When you allow yourself to be affected by someone else in a negative way this erodes your self-esteem. Your energy and state of mind becomes messy and full of confusion. You grow agitated and feelings of low self worth permeate through your body. Do not fight against the current or be affected by those around you. Recognize this when it happens and start treating yourself a bit better. Don't worry about the headlines or what people are saying. All of that is noise and does nothing to bring people together or help anything or anyone. Once you have worked on keeping the news and gossip stuff out, it will lift your state of mind into optimism. Optimism is a powerful attracter of your Universal desires.

AWAKEN YOUR INNER CHILD THROUGH JOY

Inviting laughter into your life is crucial to your well-being as it opens up your heart and awakens and unleashes your inner child. It has profound health benefits next to love. Love and joy are two of the highest energy vibrations in the universe. The entire Spirit world is bathed in the wonders of exuding those powerful feelings eternally. This is one of the biggest most recurring messages I receive. The messages they give me are sometimes repetitive if they are not being followed. The messages sound easy enough, but why is it so hard for some of us to live in that space 24/7? Many of our lives are full of stresses, toxins and disappointments. We seem to have no problem living in those conditions and choosing grief instead of harmony. This way of living is thrust upon us through osmosis and is learned behavior. You come into contact with someone who is negative or toxic and you absorb that energy. You end up taking it out on someone else and they pay that forward and so forth. Your aura and soul darkens and so does your state of mind. Soon you are behaving like that too passing it around to one another like contagion. This is what gets passed around when it should be lightheartedness, optimism, love and laughter. Many choose a path of deep anguish where they allow it to drop to a level where no one can reach them.

I sense every range of energy in the air without escape and we are indeed stressed globally. There are people out there spreading humor and joy, but it's not enough to get the tides moving fast enough. Get everyone to join in! It can be challenging when you are around others who are always mired in negativity and you cannot get away from them. They may be a partner, family member, roommates and the worst offenders, which are colleagues. The reason they are the worst offenders is because many people spend most of their days with those you work with. You cannot escape them. If that one draining apple surrounds everyone, it has the power to shift the entire mood within the work environment. Typically that one sour grape is keen on spreading it around to others who are not interested. Productivity and morale declines and it becomes an effort to get it raised again. This is carried over into our daily personal lives when we head outside, brave the streets and eventually home. You pass that energy to your friends and loved ones. You suppress or feed it by getting your hands on a toxic addiction.

Take some time out everyday to see the humor in life. Make light of situations that would otherwise be distressing. You might have put your body into a tense position or you are stuck in a rut without realizing it. You can get unstuck if you remember to have fun and unleash your inner child. You remember that kid when he was little. He saw the wonder and joy in the smallest things. When you laugh and have fun it opens up your heart Chakra, which not only invites romantic and loving situations into your life, but enables you to manifest your glorious dreams.

REMAIN OPTIMISTIC

Millions of people around the world acknowledge holidays, their birthdays or even the end of the year as a guide to see how far they have improved or progressed. They look at it as a time out to celebrate with optimism in hopes that the future will be brighter for them. It is when people will often say, "Next year will be better." If you keep saying tomorrow will be better, then you will always be one step away from happiness. Feel peacefulness today and then your challenges will lessen. We are all being forced to examine our lives in a deeper way in order to make significant changes. Many of us have been waking up in the process. This transformation you have likely been going through can make one unhappy because change is something different than what we are accustomed to. We get uncomfortable whenever there is a drastic adjustment that forces you out of your comfort zone.

There is often fear energy talk surrounding new diseases or an end of the world. These are all false fads that are beat upon society. There was never going to be an end of the world, but the negativity and the obsessive focus on that sort of talk amplifies the darker sides of the world's character. Get unstuck so you can be at a place that benefits your soul. Evaluate your beliefs, values and ways of doing things and make significant changes in your life today. By shedding all of that garbage from in and around you, you grow to be more open and receptive to the wonderful things headed your way. Be open to receive those gifts in the right spirit and start living fully today.

Chapter Five

PURIFICATION KEEPS YOUR WORLD CLEAR

*A*S YOU MAKE NECESSARY LIFE changes and adjustments that include modifications to your diet and your exercise routines, it is vital to be aware of when antagonistic energies are in your vicinity. Perhaps you head off to work everyday only to be met with a colorful array of personalities. Some are good and some are shooting invisible daggers at you. If clairvoyance is your opened clair channel, then you may see this energy. If you are more clairsentient, then you are feeling what others are pouring into you as if you are a drainpipe for their pollutants. There are various techniques that those privy to this knowledge partake in. You will need to keep an open mind about some of these methods described in this chapter. Have trust and faith that it is real and does work if you are disciplined about it and keep at it. If you have made it this far into this book then you likely have an open mind. Now I'm asking you to have faith that these methods work. Of course you can always test my Guides and Angels hypothesis before you discredit it.

CORD CUTTING

It can be challenging making the transition into a worker and warrior for the light. Sometimes there are people in your life who hold you back, get in the way or cause you grief. If there are certain people you just want to go away, then you can do so by what is called *cutting cords* or *cord cutting*. I have been doing it forever and have found it to be like magic in the way it miraculously works. With some suspects, it can take awhile to remove them out of your life, but you need to cut cords every single day with them and do not give up or stop doing it. I have seen incredible results over the course of my life doing this for myself or I would not continue to do it.

Anytime you connect and form a relationship with or to someone whether that is a family member, friend, colleague, business or love relationship, you form an etheric cord of attachment to them which clairvoyantly appears for some like a gasoline hose coming out of the other person and hooking itself onto you. If the person is needy, negative or stressful for example they are pulling high vibrational energy out of you. This feels as if someone is sucking the life force right out of you. This is a dark cord with what often appears to me like tons of spider webs wrapped around it. You know the cord has become toxic whenever that person affects you in a negative way. You will be drained, stressed out or uncomfortable whenever they are around. When the thought of them approaching you makes your stomach turn, then you can be sure there is a toxic cord that they have attached to you. This cord attachment is placed between romantic partners or potential dates as well. For example, someone who finds themselves chasing a guy who is not interested in them starts to check the guy's social networking pages daily for weeks. This is followed by a negative cord of attachment to that person. You grow to obsess over it to the point where it has taken over your life in an unhealthy way. Roommates and people who live together or those who are married form cords of attachments. This is why some couples are so in tune to how the other is feeling. Both of the lights around your souls have connected and merged. Even if one of you is living in another city, the cord is still there. This is why you need to make sure that you and your partner are aiming to experience joy in your own individual lives. If one of you is experiencing constant negativity, then the other partner can absorb that causing your cord between one another to become polluted. It can be so draining that it can even cause you to split or break up.

It's important to cut cords regularly to certain relationships due to the build up of dirty energy. This doesn't mean that you are cutting them out of your life necessarily, unless this is what you choose. You are removing the dysfunction or toxic part of the relationship. What I have discovered while cutting cords is that my Guides and Angels will either remove and eliminate that person out of my life or improve the relationship. They eliminate them if they know there is no lesson for me to learn with them. They will remove them if the lessons have been completed and yet that person is still hanging around causing me grief and holding me back. Your vibration is higher while the other person has a lower vibration. They are not intending to deplete you, but this is what is happening regardless since we are all made up of energy. If you are a sensitive person, then you are especially susceptible to the repercussions of forming an attachment to a negative and toxic person.

I cut cords every morning with certain people as part of my morning ritual. I mentally cut cords throughout the day if I need immediate intervention with someone around me. Sometimes when you work with certain people who are toxic it may be difficult to get rid of them. This is where some of the uninvited contamination happens. The second place is at home if you are living with others. This is why it so important to do your best to ask that you be guided to work or live with high vibrational people. If you are unable to live alone, request to live with similar higher vibrational people who are peace loving souls.

There are relationships that you do invite into your life where cords are formed. If you are in a loving, committed relationship with someone and you are living together, then you have formed a cord. If the relationship is based on 100% pure love and compassion, then the cord will not be as dirty, but there will be a cord. You still need to keep some form of detachment so as not to fall into a position of co-dependency as the cord can begin to get a little dusty. Those that you have formed a cord attachment with are not necessarily purposely attempting to drain your energy or spit toxins into you. They are unaware that they are doing this. You are your own barometer gauge to know how certain people affect you. Do not forget that this is your soul to protect and it is up to you to manage it. You have the assistance of God, your angels, guides and archangels within reach. All you have to do is ask for their help. You don't need to chant some complex invocation. Saying something like, *"Okay Archangel Michael I need your help with this…"* has invited him in to help. As you begin doing it, then you may find methods that you're comfortable with. You can think the word "angels" and you are heard and have invited them in.

One way I say it is, *"Please cut the cords between (so & so) and I."* I list those that I find to be toxic and draining that I have to deal with or face. Sometimes it might just be one person. Other times it's a few. There are some whom I have to cut cords with every single day until they are gone from my life or the relationship improves. Others I cut on occasion when I'm finding the union to be putting me in a negative place. There are those I love that I am close to and do not particularly want to go away, but I do not want any pain or dysfunction in the way either. For those cases I will say something like, *"Please cut the cords between (the person) and I. Only remove the toxic, fear and dysfunction from this relationship, but keep the love and lessons."* I find those relationships suddenly and drastically improve or elevate into something better. I can see and hear Archangel Michael cutting the cords with one slash of his light sword. If it is a super difficult cord that has become as hard as cement, he will continue cutting repeatedly everyday until he has removed it.

I have had cases where I'm stuck having to deal with someone whether it be a friend or colleague that is toxic, negative or a gossip—all of which I will have no part of. It can be pushed to the point where I am done with them. I have no interest and they offer nothing to me in the way of progress or growth, but merely contribute negative feelings. For those special cases I have been quite firm or even angry if nothing has been done about it. The angels are Egoless and they only see your true light and nature. They do not take anything personally such as you stomping your feet in aggression. Not that I'm advocating that you do that, but there have been times where were pushed to the edge and scream out for help. *"That's it. I want you to cut the cords between (the person's name) and I. Remove them from my life in all directions of time."* I will immediately begin to see that our connection is elevated a bit to a level that I can tolerate or they are eventually removed permanently from my life. Sometimes it's a process to extricate them from your life and its not always right away. I've seen changes and shifts happen over time. Suddenly that person is let go from their job, they decide to move on, or you have been moved away from them. The angels may have to maneuver some obstacles to make the changes you wish for that benefit your soul. In the meantime, continue cutting those cords to them everyday until they are gone or you are seeing improvement.

Working the jobs I was working at while attempting to become spiritually evolved was challenging. You might have to deal with someone who can be disconnected from reality and living in full on arrogant Ego mode. They are extremely deadly to you, your environment and well-being. You could be working at the greatest place on Earth with wonderful colleagues, but there might be that one or two people who you might just love to toss out the window. Every time you turn around they are standing there. This is where cutting cords works beautifully. These are people you have to cut cords to every single day. They may not always be extricated from your life immediately, but you may suddenly start noticing them becoming a bit more tolerable. This and all of the above have happened with me after I began cutting cords. Don't knock it until you try it. This is a lifestyle you are adopting and incorporating daily.

SHIELDING

I am a sensitive who grew to have immense social anxiety due to the abuse I endured at home growing up and yet I have to function in society in a volatile city. You take those people and give them a machine to roam around in such as a car and then you have a full-blown battlefield on the streets. The energy is worse than the anger of a murdering terrorist. This is why it is important to shield yourself. Shielding is another process to incorporate as well especially if you are a sensitive person. Sensitive people absorb energy emanating off of others like a muddy kitchen mop. Take a deep breath and call upon God and the Archangel Michael. Ask him to shield you with bright white light for protection. Mentally imagine a cocoon of white light surrounding you. This will keep out those nasty pests that insist on entering your field. The people you work for or whom you are around regularly can be the greatest people, but even great people get moody, agitated and out of line. You sense this energy and vibration and it suddenly lowers yours. See the innocence and humor in other people and do not let their drama and moods affect you.

Envision different colored shields of light surrounding you. These heavenly lights can be layered together or on its own. They last up to 12 hours so you will need to do it daily as needed.

> » *White*—Strongest light that protects you. Nothing can penetrate this shield.
> » *Rose/Pink*—Offers protection while allowing only the love to enter your auric field.
> » *Emerald Green*—Heals you in all ways such as physically, mentally or emotionally.
> » *Violet*—Assists in raising your spiritual gifts and psychic sight.
> » *Gold*—Powerful. Brings in God's love and light. Blasts away and repels all traces of negative thoughts and your lower self from your mind and body.

Remember to ask for help from your Guides and Angels. Even if you've been asking and haven't seen results and are losing faith—keep on asking and putting that energy out there. They are not ignoring you. If it is not happening right away there is a reason, but it will happen. There are obstacles and barriers that they are removing that are in the way to get you to that place you want to be in. You need to pay attention and listen for the signs that they might be giving you as well. They may be answering and advising you, but you are not paying any attention to it as you're expecting the answer to take a different form. If you are getting a repetitive sign that happens more than three times and benefits your higher self and overall well-being, then you are receiving divine messages. They want you to be at peace and to have enough time and resources to be able to focus and work on your life purpose. They don't want you to be stuck at a dead end job struggling to make ends meet. Start working with your team today to improve your life one step at a time.

DISENGAGE FROM ANGUISH

Steer clear of everyone else's irrelevant drama. It doesn't do you or anybody any good to get involved with someone's Ego. Someone else's stuff is not yours to absorb. You cannot learn other people's lessons for them. Don't respond, ignore them and walk away. As human souls, we do not take enough breaks and the few holidays we are all given off we spend it tired or wasted. When everyone is back to what they might consider to be the grind and the mundane, they are reminded of how unhappy they are with some part of their life. *(i.e. job, relationships, finances)* The edgy feelings they had of feeling stuck rise once again. The slightest issue can be blown out of proportion and you might be caught in the line of that fire. Remove yourself from the racket if you find yourself being a target of someone else's blow up. Always revert back to focusing on you and your higher path. Become the calm in the eye of the hurricane. As for those acting out, they are discontent with where they are at and they are receiving nudges from their own Spirit team to make some long awaited adjustments to their life. That is not anyone's problem to solve, but their own. You want to disengage and detangle yourself from other people's misery. This doesn't mean you are to be cold hearted. You can still be supportive and compassionate by not attaching yourself to their drama.

ETHERIC CREATURES GNAWING ON MY LIGHT

The same way that spiders are sensitive to vibrations on their web, I am equally sensitive to the vibrations in and around me. If you are a sensitive or in tune to Spirit you will likely know what I am talking about. I cannot be in crowded environments. I cannot bear obtrusive noises such as traffic sounds or garbage cans banging around. Naturally I assume no one is a fan, but my not liking it borders beyond what the general public can likely tolerate. I often slam my windows shut for a few minutes, or cover my ears when a siren is going by, or a super loud plane is flying overhead. Having clairaudience heightens every sound around you beyond the norm too. It can be unbearable. The only loud sounds I can tolerate are music. Music is the sound that connects us to the other side.

When my spiritual sight opened up after I had rid myself of negative ways of living, I found that I had a steady link and connection to the Spirit world. This was also when I began hearing what sounded like chattering. I know it was not Heaven as the sound was creepy and uncomfortable. It would cut in and out as if it were a bad cell phone reception. It wasn't long before I started seeing these dark insects in my peripheral vision. My guides wanted me to know that due to my sudden increase in psychic activity I was attracting a number of skittering little etheric creatures that nibble on positive energy.

The more you study and grow your psychic abilities, the brighter the light that you give off becomes—both in your aura and as your soul footprint. These etheric creatures feed off of random positive energies. As your light grows they are attracted to your vicinity. These creatures make a little skittering noise like squirrels chattering. They were distracting me on a level that I wasn't fully aware of immediately and this caused a subtle change in my focus. These annoying little pests would break up my concentration and keep my subconscious mind from working on the walls and barriers I erected to protect myself from emotional damage. My Guides and Angels explained that I had full knowledge of suitable aura protection methods, but that I was not using them consistently enough. This allowed these little pests to get in. I used to be lazy when it came to shielding and protecting my soul. Part of me did not believe in it until I had invited in an entire army of negative pests. Don't underestimate the value of this protection, because if these little pests can penetrate your armor, some bigger bad bods can do more than just distract you. This is in no ways meant to scare you. No one is in immediate danger from anything on this level. As you continue to study and grow your psychic abilities, you can become the target of larger entities that require bigger feeding stations, and this can get to be pretty draining.

A certain level of my consciousness was distracted by the ebb and flow of the spiritual work that I was doing more of. Combine this with the annoying little pests that were nibbling at my energy. I was not quite as aware of who/what is and was coming into my immediate path during my major spiritual transition. I could hear the little skittering noises of these psychic pests, which can be likened to that of a buzzing bee. When you hear them it will confirm their presence for you. If you choose to take action without the confirmation, then you need to bump up your protection visualizations morning and night. This can be as simple as envisioning an armor of golden light protection around you and make that absolutely impermeable. Visualize yourself completely surrounded and utterly sealed off to anything except 100% positive energy. Believe that you are protected against all incoming energies that try to drain your psychic, mental and emotional energies. Affirm three times each session that you are protected and armored against these intrusions. See yourself as unbreakable!

The white light energizes whatever is in it. If it's an entity made up of darkness that is negative and evil, then the white light will literally cause an explosion when it meets its opposite. The entity will disappear and leave. I had experimented with this by pushing a few of those little mosquito-type chattering annoyances into it as you would push something in the water away from you. They would pop like popcorn to demonstrate their change in polarity. If you are going to grow your own light and expand your consciousness, awareness, place and work in this world, you will attract those who will try to stop you from doing this. It doesn't mean you're in danger. It just means you need to be aware of this and practice safe psychic study. Nothing is free as there is always an exchange of energy for energy. The more light you give off, the more darkness you attract. The more you know and grow, the more attractive you and the light you give off becomes. It's like putting a teensy low watt bulb on your porch and having a few moths attracted to it. It is that versus putting a 100 watt bulb out there and having every single insect of all varieties within a 10-block radius coming to gobble up the heat, light, and any other food they can find there. You're drawing in more of those energy eaters.

Regardless of where I or you came from, we are here in our bodies now. My higher self and soul grew to be so bright and intense with blasting white light that all the darkness was extremely attracted to me. Think of it as mosquitoes buzzing around a tasty human wanting to take a little drink of the yummy blood. They are dark bugs drawn to a blazing flame. I had become dinner and those nasty dark beings wanted to get in and drain my delicious positive white light energy from me. This is why it's important for you to cleanse yourself with white light and seal your aura with gold light. Having the intention and visualizing this can do the job. You can find various instructions online on how to do this and ask for guidance to the right way to do it. You'll know it's the right one when you experience positive vibes about what you've stumbled upon. Once you build that better suit of armor around your soul, then you will be fully able to concentrate on your own interior work, knowing that you are safe from all nefarious incomers.

The brighter your light shines, the more you draw in negative energy. If you are in the middle of a spiritual awakening or transition yourself, then you are at the beginning of an important journey. Don't rush it because it takes years and lifetimes to master. You have all been truly blessed with your own gifts and abilities whether you are aware of them or not. What you do with them in this lifetime is up to you, but you have the opportunity to do great good in the world in the subtlest of ways by allowing your light to shine in a way that does no harm to you or anyone else. That light can infuse everything you do. By learning about it and yourself, you will let more light come into the world. The world always needs more light to keep the balance between the light and the darkness. If you never do anything else, but let your loving energy shine through to the world, that will be enough to help combat all the evil in the world.

LIFE PURPOSE

Your life purpose is an interesting dichotomy in figuring out what it is. It can be what you love doing more than anything in the world. It can also be whatever makes you angry or riles you up. For example, someone who is always getting upset or angry when people throw trash in the ocean. They were meant to come here to do something about it such as joining in with Greenpeace, start a blog or mobilize to clean up the oceans. This is their life purpose.

To turn your hobby into a career, take actions towards it daily. You can do this in baby steps. Spend at least thirty minutes a day absolving yourself in whatever it is you want to accomplish. If you are working on a book, then spend at least thirty minutes each day writing a page. The universe will meet you tenfold in manifesting your dreams. When you are working on what you love, then it doesn't feel like a drag. You may be working at a job you're not all that happy with, but when you have something to look forward to at the end of the day, then it raises your vibration. This opens up the door for the universe to step in and meet you half way. You'll be that much closer to having your dream come true. If you keep at it, then eventually that love will be your career. It will bring in enough financially that you're able to quit the job you're unhappy with. Ones hobby or love is often connected to their life purpose.

When you are not at your job, what do you enjoy doing on your off time? What is your hobby? Is it painting? Is it singing or playing the guitar? Your hobby is not surfing the internet, heading to the bar with friends or shopping for clothes. Those are called distractions, time wasters and addiction feeders. Your hobby is an activity that you enjoy doing on your own. It's one that gives you an added skill or knowledge around a certain area that gives you pleasure. Your hobby is what you want to turn into a career.

Let's look at a couple of well known entertainers. Bruce Springsteen has been playing his guitar since he was a teenager. When he was playing the guitar in those days it was his hobby and something he enjoyed doing. He was able to transition that hobby into a full time career that has lasted a lifetime. When Madonna was a teenager she enjoyed dancing. This was her hobby. She took classes and looked for work that would enable her to incorporate her love for dancing. She was able to broaden that into an even bigger career that has also lasted a lifetime. Music entertainers bring joy to the world and Heaven applauds this.

Many people who are working at jobs that are not surrounding their hobby are more likely to be unhappy than those who are. I have been shown that those who are unhappy with their jobs tend to reach for addictions like alcohol or food more than those who are happy. Some of them reach for addictions like a caffeine fix mid-day. They will pop pills to sleep at night and then have caffeine or an energy jolt to get them started every morning. You take something at night to calm down and sleep, then something energetic to get you going. The days where they are not at their job be it the weekend or a vacation day, they are less likely to reach for these substances. This is a clue that you are unhappy at your job, but are convincing yourself that this is just the way it is.

What don't you have that you wished you had? Is it a great career, love or good health? Are you at a job you enjoy, but wish you were working at your dream career? Take time each day to work on your career while you still work your day job. You will be that much closer to obtaining your dream. You will also have something to look forward to at the end of the day when you leave your job. When you head home to spend at least thirty minutes towards your hobby you are devoting time towards your passion.

If you keep making excuses such as, 'I'm too tired, I never have enough time', then you push your dream that much further away from you. The right time may never come unless you take control over your life by working this hobby into your schedule. I've worked two full time jobs that include my regular job and my career. It can be done if everything in your entire being loves this hobby. You can turn this into a career if it is work that you are interested in doing.

How would you like to get paid for doing work that you love and have fun doing? It does not feel like work if it is something you love. This is also a sign that it is your life purpose. You should never quit your regular job until your hobby has turned into something lucrative enough that you know you will be able to survive.

DIVINE TIMING

Heaven wants us to be at peace and not suffer, but they can only help us achieve this when we invite them into our lives and begin working with them. After I began testing them out and was receiving incredible results in the process, only then was I wowed and a believer. Some may call it coincidence, but how can you call something coincidence that happens consistently every time you ask for something over a period of decades? The more you work with them, then the more your life begins to change in positive ways. You find that your friendships and relationships begin to shift and improve. Those that were toxic and negative to begin with suddenly start exiting your life or you find you are drifting apart. It is not that you are repelling them, but they are repelling you! What once attracted you to them is no longer the case. You no longer feel a rush out of gossip, negativity, addictions or destruction anymore. This process can take what seems a long while, but know that it is all happening and in motion. The angels are working with you on eliminating these people that no longer serve your higher purpose and your vibration rises in the process. As that happens, you find that you are finally living the life you always wanted or heading rather quickly towards it.

There is always some turmoil or tantrums whenever change happens with human souls. Trust that the changes have a greater benefit to you in the end. Have patience and faith that it will. Everyone wants things now-now-now and I'm certainly no exception. You can make things easier on yourself when you know that there are good reasons for things not happening right away and trusting that it will. There is that word again: Trust. This is a word the angels remind us of everyday. Patience. That's another one. Sometimes there are lessons that you need to learn before you are shown the next step. Take a step back and pause. Go within and inside yourself for the answer. This is also known as your intuition. See what answers come to you on the situation you are questioning. Ask to have your Ego and lower self removed as you tune into the messages being relayed to you. You will discover why there has been no change in your life yet. You may find that your lessons have been learned and there is nothing more to gain, but the delay in movement is because your Guides and Angels are working diligently behind the scenes to make it happen for you. There are circumstances that need to occur first on the other end before anything can happen.

An example might be, let's say that you are unhappy in the apartment you are living in and have asked for help in finding a new place of residence. You can't understand what the delay is in receiving that help. What you may not even realize is that you have an idea of what apartment you're going to move into, but your Spirit team sees an even better scenario. They see you in an actual home of your own in an area you have only dreamt about. Yet, you deny this possibility because you don't believe you could ever own a home in this current market and with your financial status. They see something bigger entirely up ahead for you. They see a big sell with a project they have been assisting you with for some time. You don't see the potential financial gain, but they do which enables you to purchase that home. They may see you moving in with a potential love partner you've been dating. This move takes place in an entirely different part of town. If you jump towards something out of impatience you could potentially throw your path off course and cause an even greater delay.

Your Ego is fixated on nabbing something immediately and talks you into jumping. It sounds like a great idea to you at first. You later discover that you wished you had exercised more patience for the real excellent stuff. Delays are for a good reason so that other pieces of the puzzle can be put into place and maneuvered into something far greater than you imagined. When you meditate, take pause or even daydream you connect to your Spirit team. You can see what they are currently working on for you. Our Guides and Angels always see us as being more capable than we see ourselves. If you are receiving something that seems so far-fetched, then it is important that you remember to have faith and trust in it.

THE WHITE LIGHT

White light is the color of spirit, purity, transformation and completion. There was and is no end to this world. We have all been changing. We have been bringing our previous lives to a close by shedding anything and everything that has blocked or prevented us from welcoming in new and better circumstances. Some of us do not have a choice. The universe is forcing it on all of humanity. There are some who may stomp their feet or sulk, as change can feel uncomfortable. Our own Spirit teams are individually assisting us all more than ever to make this change. They are also bringing souls to you in human form to enlighten you. The answers we need are coming from the source and the white light within each of us. Tune into it, embrace it and follow it. It has always been there and it has always been this way since you came to being, but this has been kicked up a notch and is targeted globally. Many people are looking and longing for answers. Some of them are seeking out some form of spirituality since it is more compassionate and open hearted. We cannot wander around oblivious in our lives anymore and nor can we can ignore it. This white light is growing around the globe and more people of this white light are being born to usher it along so that it can be spread like wildfire.

Here is a brief cheat sheet to give you an idea on how to tell the difference between some of the stuff that raises your vibration and what can and will lower it:

Raises Vibration

» Exercise
» Healthy Foods
» Surrounding yourself w/ positive people
» Optimism
» Smiling
» Cuddling/Hugging
» Expressing Love

» Praying/Affirmations
» Nature (i.e. relaxing, walking, meditating)
» Music/Singing/Dance

» Grateful/ Gratitude
» Love Relationships
» Breathing techniques

» Water
» Creativity (i.e. art projects)
» Forgiveness
» Compassion
» Experiencing Peace

Lowers Vibration

» Alcohol
» Drugs
» Poor lifestyle choices

» Stress/Depression
» Coffee/Caffeine
» Sugar
» Foods high in fat, sugar, sodium, cholesterol
» Hate/Judgment
» Gossip/Complaining

» Negativity (i.e. fear, emotion, anger, guilt)
» Revenge/Gloating
» Unruly Ego
» Being around negative people
» Time Wasters (i.e. internet surfing, phone apps to meet people, games, bars, clubs)

Chapter Six

FRIENDSHIPS CHANGE AS YOU EVOLVE

WHEN YOU WALK ON A higher spiritual path your Guides and Angels will start to repel those you need to stay away from while bringing in new people who are aiming for spiritual growth or who are already living in the light. Changes in your friendships are a normal process for those that are frequently evolving. You find that you no longer have the same interests as those you had considered once close. When my vibration had risen to an astronomical degree from my previous way of life, I discovered that those I had once connected with were either headed down a path I had no interest in or seemed content to stay exactly where they are with no need for improvement. The interests they had were purely based on a superficial level. Many of them were also prone to spending their days drinking, experimenting with drugs or being a regular fixture in a bar. That used to be who I was, but I was evolving so rapidly I could not even fake my interest in those activities.

I chose to create a relationship with God and my Spirit team daily, working and communicating with them. This enabled me to not only improve my life, but help others as well. Having an understanding of where we came from has assisted me navigating through the often challenging roads were often faced with as human souls. I chose to be mindful and cautious of who I allowed around me and what I was ingesting into my body including foods and other addictions. This was not only because my interest in it was dropping, but having those around you who operate on a lower vibration will contaminate your aura and own positive energy. This is a perfect example of why psychic readers or anyone who works with the general public should practice shielding themselves.

I was hesitant to discussing my rising spiritual interests or in opening up about how I knew certain things for fear of ridicule with just anyone. I did not want to announce or say the words of where I was getting my accurate information about them from. I assumed that the majority of people around me were mostly atheists or who had no belief in God, a higher power, the light or whatever one associates God to be. The main reason I assumed this was they preferred living a toxic path. They had never uttered a spiritual word as long as I had known them. This does not bother me of course, because I do not discredit good friendships simply because of a different belief system. As long as both parties are open and accepting of the other person's way of life, then there is no reason to not be friends. You have to have a high level of maturity to be able to be friends with those who have differing opinions and beliefs. You naturally would limit and keep your philosophical discussions to a minimum. However, there is a difference if they are partaking in certain vices that are no longer conducive to your overall well-being.

For others around me I noticed that if it was not about sex or something superficial, then they could not be more bored or uninterested. This started to limit my friendships as we live in a world that is hyper-media focused. They may not be all that interested in anything beyond superficiality as this is what they have allowed their communities and peers to raise them on. It keeps them distracted and disconnected from knowing who they are and why they are here to begin with. When there is no room for anything else, then as a spiritual person you lose interest. If I posted something on my social networking page in the realms of spirituality there would be one or two bad apples that would comment something patronizing about it or make a joke. I was around those that were either spiritually open or sexually open. If I posted something in either category I feared mockery from one or the other. I felt that I could not truly be myself and there appeared to be no room for any of it. I moved into a place of wanting to remove all traces of me on social networking sites, but then my higher self grabbed hold of the reigns to say, 'Wait a minute. This is my life and I'll post what I want. If you don't like it then remove yourself or I'll remove you.' I had to put my foot down and remove hundreds of people that I knew were going to have judgment towards the spiritual stuff or the sex stuff. These same people were around when I used to be slightly superficial myself. I changed and never reverted back. We are all unique individuals with varying concepts to share or teach. My Spirit team let me know that the right people who are more aligned with my new beliefs and who are open to all of it would be attracted to me.

LONELINESS

Loneliness is a common complaint among so many people I have discovered. They express feelings of loneliness and a lack of having friendships. This is especially the case if you are going through a spiritual or major transition of some kind. The spiritual community is an open, accepting and loving group of bright souls. It is still not easy for one to make friendships whenever there is any kind of transition in your life to begin with. If you are frequently evolving, then you are going through many shifts and transitions in your life. This process weeds out many of your current friendships. You must be comfortable being alone and with yourself before you can attract in new friendships. This is the same concept as searching for a soul mate. You cannot go searching for a soul mate or friendships. All REAL relationships and connections happen when you are not looking for them. They always come to you naturally and effortlessly at the right time.

Loneliness is the human condition. You came into this world alone and you will leave this world alone. When you were born you were a perfect well rounded human soul experiencing joy, peace and contentment. It was society and those that raised you that inflicted all sorts of nonsense onto your soul causing you to experience negative feelings such as loneliness. Loneliness is an emptiness that cannot be cured or filled up by another human soul. It also should not be filled up with addictions. That emptiness is so vast it would be outlandish to place that responsibility on another person to fill. What you are craving is God's love. You will also not attract in the right kind of friendships in a state of loneliness or boredom. You will attract in those that are similar or far worse leaving you to fall into a deeper despair. Get happy and productive first and allow the right friendships to come in on their own time. You will be content with this new you that you will not even have the time or notice when or if the right friendships have shown up yet. Find personal hobbies and interests to occupy your time off so that you are not lying in bed with a beer feeling deep loneliness. Ask your Guides and Angels to remove those feelings of loneliness and help you to experience profound joy.

You will also need to look at where you are hoping to find new friendships. Are you going to the bars to find these new friendships? Many people do this only to end up being disappointed. When they do meet someone at a place like that, the friendships are short lived. You are meeting those that likely partake in the same escapism as you do. What happens when you are friends with someone who does that? You both fall into the bell jar together delaying yourself from achieving the life you have always dreamed about while drinking constantly. Bars are a place where many dark entities lurk. These are spirits that avoided the light when they passed away. They attach themselves to many of the drinking patrons permanently or for a prolonged period of time. They prompt that person to continuously drink and even do hard drugs indefinitely. They get them to make poor life choices. This is not in judgment as I will be the first to raise my hand to say that I used to love hanging in bars. It was where the drinks were! There is a difference between going to a bar with a friend once in a blue moon for a drink versus going to a bar weekly or even daily! Many of the friendships you make if any are with those who love you in that moment of high intoxication, but their feelings suddenly shift when they wake up the next morning feeling gross, moody, lethargic and unfit. The only way to get rid of the feeling is to continue drinking. It's a cycle until you put your foot down that you need to keep it in moderation or give it up completely. It is no surprise that many who fit this description are starving for real friendships. You cannot attract quality friendships while in a state of addictions. You will only bring in more like you who are not the stable friendships you desire.

I had a friend warn someone to never use the word *bored* around me. This is true because there is always something to do. To begin curbing your feelings of loneliness and boredom, find out what your true hobbies and interests that make you happy are. Do you enjoy regular walks on the beach, certain sports, road trips or creative pursuits? The key is to choose an activity that is not negative or toxic, but rather productive and uplifting. This is where you are likely to find quality friendships. If you love painting in your spare time, then consider taking a course on painting at a trade school or college. It does not matter if you already know how to do it, because it will get your energy out there in the right places. You will be spending several months or many weeks with the same people who have a like minded interest. They are more apt to be quality people who are productive in their lives as well. You are also spending your free time wisely by engaging in something you love doing. This raises your vibration to a more joyful level, which attracts more good things into your life including great friendships!

WE ARE ALL TEACHERS

As you shift into a more spiritually minded person you appreciate the connections you make with those around you. This can be people you don't know, a friendship, relationship or an acquaintance. We all learn something from someone that crosses paths with us because everyone is a teacher. This can be someone you have only met for as little as a minute. Take a look at the various people you have crossed paths with in the past. It can even be someone that cuts you off in traffic. What could they possibly have had to teach you, you might ask. How about patience? Perhaps you are being taught to not allow the little things to affect you and to stay detached from any kind of traumatic crisis. Look at all the close relationships you have had that are long passed. It is easy for us to have disdain towards certain past relationships where one might have been hurt, but I don't regret any of my relationships, even the bad ones when I look back. There was knowledge I had to gain while in them as we are all meant to gain something of substance in relation to our growth. We attracted in that person at that particular time and it was designed to be of benefit for the both of us. There comes a time while in a friendship or love relationship with someone where one or both of you have served your purpose and the point becomes moot. This is when you know it is time to move on. With certain relationships, such as romantic, there can be two people who spend this entire lifetime together and act as partners in crime. They are evolving together and facing in the same direction. They gain knowledge while together as well as with those they come into contact with outside of the relationship.

DISSOLVING FRIENDSHIPS

Your true friends never ridicule or make fun of you, but support you. They don't place unnecessary demands on you or your time. They are flexible and know how you operate and accept this. If you have a friend that has been consistently upset over something you do or don't do, then its time to consider distancing yourself temporarily or dissolving the union altogether if it continues. You both have different values and what you expect from the other. If you were once seeing eye-to-eye and facing the same direction, you have both now hit a fork in the road and are embarking on separate paths with different views and interests. The purpose of your friendship has been fulfilled.

If you are negative and a gossip, then you will attract that same type of person to you. When you grow and walk a larger path, you will find that you can no longer relate to those people you initially attracted in. In fact, you find them to be energy zappers where you are drained after having a phone conversation with them. You become fully aware of your surroundings and how they have contributed to your negative state. You realize how miserable you are with them only to discover that you played a part in it too.

The only way to start attracting friendships with greater people is to begin the process of improving yourself first. There will be a transition period that could last anywhere from one to three years as you work on yourself in a big way. During this transition, some of your previous friendships will begin fading and newer improved friendships will gradually come to you. You may find that there will be some friendships that may be difficult to dissolve. These friends may have been the biggest energy zappers of them all. They feed on you like a vampire. They have their clutches in you and have no desire to ever let go. Pay no mind or attention to this. It's not your responsibility to provide happiness to anyone. Ask Archangel Michael mentally, out loud or in writing to assist you in peacefully dissolving those friendships and relationships that have been consistently causing you grief.

I had friends that I was not comfortable with discussing my spiritual awakening and the profound changes that were happening within me. You never share your dreams with those you have to convince. If people are critical, then it can shut down your Heavenly connections and block your communication with God. Their ridicule will affect your self-esteem and lower your vibration. I found that I had friends that might not understand my spiritual beliefs, but were delighted to hear about it. Most people find that they are curious or fascinated by it because there is something about it that reminds them of who they once were in the Spirit world. It triggers a memory and offers them comfort. They may be at a point in their life where nothing around them matters. They are trapped in their body unable to connect to anything. There were many who had never uttered a word of spirituality, but grew to be interested in that realm after hearing my teachings. They miraculously expanded into that world too.

I found that my interests in certain friendships and people were changing. Doors were opening and relationships were shifting by ending or improving. It was a period of adjustment and I would have previously approached that kicking and screaming, but instead it was a peaceful transition. I did find that those that were part of religious institutions had taken more of a liking to me than atheists did. Even though religious and spiritual beliefs are different in certain areas, we all found some common denominators when it comes to circumstances like an afterlife, God and angels. I had sat with a religious couple over a dinner once. They later had commented to someone that we mutual knew at how awestruck they were with me. They were blown away and moved by the spirituality I spoke about. There is familiar ground in varying belief systems if people remain open.

I've also made enemies for being open about my beliefs. I've had people who have volunteered to write me out of the blue through a social networking page, "Wow, I realized that I don't like you at all." They would then delete and block me. They were surprisingly atheists who I thought would be more open than someone who was religious. I found the opposite to be the case. You ignore it and forge on with your purpose in merging with the Light. The Light will ensure that all of your needs are met and that you are around good-hearted people who understand you and who you are comfortable around. The angels will deter those who are a danger for you to be around and extricate them out of your vicinity. Their energy is toxic and Ego based and you being a sensitive and in tune to your surroundings will soak that up like a dirty rag. Meanwhile in the works are greater more important people who operate from a higher place and are being drawn to you as you make the shift onto a higher level of consciousness. It takes quite a bit of time because you're growing and evolving at a rapid pace and there are people who are exiting your life much slower.

You will be hesitant to dissolving certain friendships because you do care about them and the good times you had, but at the same time they are not welcoming or responsive towards your new beliefs. They are living unhealthy lives that no longer jive with who you are becoming. You may choose to make yourself less available to them until they have been moved into your acquaintance box. Before you know it you will be communicating less and less. Some of these friendships and relationships might be with people who are heavily into negative substances and addictions. Long before you've made that spiritual shift, you might have already been working on your lifestyle, which includes what you consume and shove into your body. You will find that the new friendships you make are with people who are open to what you believe in even if they do not partake in it or fully understand it. Those unions are more beautiful, loving and better than you could ever have imagined with anybody else. They are pure and full of light. You create a bigger uplifting energy when you are together. You have surpassed a superficial mundane existence and expanded your consciousness even more.

My friendships changed to a great degree when my communications with my guides opened up. Some shifted comfortably with my heightened interest. They effortlessly accepted that this is the new me and not some whimsical fly by hobby. I have eternally changed and continue to do so. This is the same concept as those that claim to be born again Christians. They might have run into friendships that no longer shared their beliefs or talked it down. One of the differences may be is that my reason for letting people go is because they are not serving my highest good. They may not support me and instead ridicule my interests. Archangel Michael is by my side on a daily basis and he extracts those people from my vicinity before I'm even aware that they are close. I discuss some of the main Archangels and their specialties in more detail in a later chapter in this book.

The spiritual transition I was making was empowering, but there was an immense amount of alone time because I was no longer interested in those I was previously connecting with. I was in an area where there were only certain types of people I would experience a connection with. If I felt isolated before, then I felt inaccessible and disconnected from everyone during the transition. This is a normal and typical part of the process where your personal life might appear to be unfulfilling. You are removing your previous old way of life in order to bring in new people on your level. I would continue to be approached and many would express great interest towards me, but I felt empty with other people. I would wonder how long in with them before it was time for me to mention my spiritual interests and how quickly the judgment or skepticism would fall over their face. I knew that I would have to remain in the spiritual closet until I knew it was safe to open up about it with the right people. It generally was not that long before I would know whether or not someone would be in a place to hear it and understand. I had discussed it with certain friends who I assumed were spiritually inclined, but found that it would go through one ear and out the other. This would be the case whenever I would share the profound changes that were happening with me. It was as if they did not buy it or believe it, so they opted to ignore that it was said. I could tell by meeting with someone who would be open to it after a few sentences spoken from their mouth.

I knew love and romance was going to be more of a challenge, as this person would have to completely understand. They would not have to partake in it or do the things I do, but that person would have to be open minded, supportive and loving about it. What I do and what I experience with this is not up for a debate. I knew there would be no way I could be involved with a non-believer because this is something I do everyday now. I would need to communicate with the one I am with and I would have to be open about that. How could I do that if it would be subjected to ridicule? If you find yourself in that predicament, then ask your Guides and Angels to send you someone who is totally open and receptive to what you do without judgment and who is walking a spiritual path of some kind. This was not the only reason I chose to be alone. The portal was open into this new way of life and I was fascinated and immersed in study and research as I perfected the gifts I already had.

Never divulge your dreams or deepest interests to just anyone and especially not to someone you suspect to be a negative naysayer. Guard your dreams and aspirations with delicacy. Don't blurt out your closest secrets to just anyone. You can tell by the response you get from someone whether or not they back you or if they are operating purely on Ego. One who supports and coaxes you on your dream is the real deal. Someone who is always belittling you or responding negatively to your dreams or your work should be dissolved out of your life. With all of the wonderful people in the world it's important to not waste one minute with someone who has issues about you or is jealous of you and the attention you receive.

I am impossible to control, which is another sign of spiritual progress. I act and function in complete independence. I do not follow the crowd and have always had my own views, which at times are unpopular. I do not pay any mind to how others feel about it including those close to me. I have had friends in the past that were uncomfortable that I own my life. They would find some way to undercut something about me. They would say it as a backhanded compliment as if I wouldn't notice. I do not become friends with unsupportive belittling people. I do not act that way in return, because I live in a higher frequency than they do. Many of them I had disbanded out of my life. I am not friend's with people who exude those traits today. My detector is incredibly tuned that I can tell if that is someone's personality up front. They do not get far with me. There were those who were unaware of their lack of tact and I would continue to keep them around, but not hesitate to correct them on their naivety. Only allow those with the highest of integrity near you.

Friendships have to be earned and should never be immediate. This applies to romantic relationships as well. We attract friendships to us the way we attract anything, through the laws of attraction. If you are at a certain level of growth you will only attract those that mirror your intent. If you're consuming negative substances such as drugs and alcohol, what types of people do you think you're going to attract in? You're not going to attract someone walking in the light. If you find that you have on that rare occasion, then there is a reason for it. The reason is that person who is a spiritual being was guided to you by Heaven. They see you are ready to grow out of your current phase. The wonderful spiritual being is your teacher and will not be around you forever if you abuse it. When they leave you prematurely, then you may continue down your path of self-sabotage and destruction. You are given an Earth Angel to cross your path to help you to wake up and progress your soul. There are many out there threading through the world to get you to wake up and walk the path of love, joy and peace. It is important to recognize who they are.

THE HUMAN HEART:
RELATIONSHIPS, SOUL MATES
AND TWIN FLAMES

EVERYONE IS INTERESTED IN LOVE and relationships whether they like to admit it or not. Even the most hardened human soul has fantasized about having a love interest or a partner in crime. One of the main reasons we are all here is to love and to learn how to love. This is not just in intimate relationships, but with everyone we come into contact with. We must accept someone else's differences in the way that they choose to set up their life as long as it is not harming someone else or themselves. It is in our nature to want to help others out of love even if it is in the form of tough love. Relationships have grown to be more complicated over the years. Society has imposed particular values and rules when it comes to how relationships are formed and should be. There was a time when interracial marriage was banned. Now there are laws on the books allowing same sex couples to marry or the law is banning them from marrying. There was a point when divorce was seen as something sinful and you would be ostracized by society permanently. If you committed adultery, you would have to wear the scarlet letter "A" as you made your way into town so everyone could see that you had committed a big no-no. You were forced to walk in shame upon judgmental and critical eyes. Divorce and adultery still go on today, but you're not forced to wear a button that says, "I'm a cheater."

Cheating is still frowned upon, as it brands someone's character as untrustworthy. Most of us hope that those that are in our lives can control themselves and can be trusted. You cannot be with someone around the clock even if you live with them. The angels do not judge someone who has cheated and nor do they brand them with a label. They see the underlying cause within that individual that prompts them to stray. They want to assist them in healing the source or fundamental origin that leads that person to seek out false fulfillment in toxic or harmful ways. They can only do so when that person has acknowledged that they want some help. If they do not feel they are doing anything wrong, then there is little they or anyone else can do to help them. All you have to do is have great intention or an outpouring request to the universe that you need some assistance. You will have an angel or guide who will work with you in ridding yourself of certain temptations. These uncontrollable desires cause hurt and pain in your relationships and ultimately to yourself.

Divorce is something that people in most cultures have come to understand and accept over the centuries. Your Guides and Angels will never urge you to leave your partner unless that person is emotionally, verbally or physically abusive. They are all about working on your union since there is no such thing as a perfect relationship. There are going to be times when you feel misunderstood or are not being heard by your partner. This is your Ego that is stomping its feet demanding more attention. Often times when a couple hits a roadblock in their relationship, the answer is typically simpler than they are able to see. The angels understand that some couples grow apart or stop seeing eye-to-eye. This is why they have performed miraculous interventions with couples that have reached a place where they are no longer speaking to one another. After the angels have intervened, that couple begins to see each other in a new light and are able to rekindle what they once had. They had done the same for me when I had asked them for assistance.

There are cases where there is no other solution within the relationship except to dissolve it amicably and peacefully. Every union's issues vary from one couple to the next. The bottom line is that relationships and love are a big deal to many people. We want to connect to others in a positive way and it disheartens us when it fails or does not go according to expectations or plan. The angels watch you and your partner wrestle with hurt. They see the many miscommunications going on between the both of them. The angels see the answer that can correct the misunderstanding and want to help you to see it too. Once you reach that place you achieve bliss within the partnership again.

There are those who prefer to be a lone wolf, but even they have moments where they wish there was someone in their life to do things with or communicate to on occasion. There are committed relationships that work where both partners do not live with one another or they only see each other irregularly. There are also many who prefer to live together almost immediately and often prematurely. Your Guides and Angels understand that it is a human need to want someone to share your life's journey with. This is why they work with those who request their help to bring in a loving, committed partner.

We all have certain requirements in a relationship with someone else that isn't always fulfilled. For instance, you may crave a passionate, sex life with your partner while they look at you as someone to hang out and do things with. They may not be romantic, passionate or have a desire for the kind of hearts and flowers love that you want. This can ultimately end a relationship if issues as simple as this are not accepted or addressed. The way to avoid an ending is to accept that this is where you are both different and then put in an effort to meet the other half way. If you crave that passion around the clock, then ease up on that need, while the partner that does not have a desire for it should put in some time to be passionate with their partner that wants it.

Bigger issues that cause relationship break ups are where one person wants children and the other does not. Many issues can be worked around to an extent, but these types of major issues should be resolved during the dating process, rather than when you are knee-deep years into the relationship. Many jump immediately into a relationship without truly knowing who they are joining in with. Before I ventured into other territory in my work such as spirituality, I was writing about love, dating, relationships and sex. This is an area that I seemed to be born knowing about. I already had a grasp of the human condition and gained additional guidance and messages from my Guides and Angels as well. Because of this and through my life experiences, I have successfully assisted and navigated many people through the challenges and questions revolving around their love and relationship lives.

DYSFUNCTIONAL RELATIONSHIPS

We attract people that are similar to us or who we have something to learn from or teach to. I am not going to be attracting the bad drug-dealing user I was at age twenty-two. I had spent my life from the time I was a kid wanting to be in a committed, love relationship where I would grow and evolve with one person. By the time I was sixteen, I was ready to settle down. Of course it didn't happen quite so simply. I did not have a positive view of successful relationships as I grew up amidst adultery and violent or negative unions. Spirit embedded the true long-term view of love relationships in me at birth. I had been disappointed and victimized to a high degree that I stopped trusting everybody. All I wanted seemed simple enough and yet I could not figure out why that was incredibly difficult for others to do. The basic necessities of life are love and security.

Some of us are more flawed than others and operate mostly on Ego first. We must be fully aware of how we treat others and it should be with respect and love. As a result of my upbringing, I grew to be suspicious of anyone who attempted to get close to me. I would create self-fulfilling prophecies such as how long is this one going to last? How long before this person takes off in search of something else? I wonder what they want from me or do they have an ulterior motive. I came to the conclusion that was the norm. I had not realized that I was attracting the same type of person into me repeatedly and not everyone is the same. As a super, passionate hot-blooded guy I would choose to get serious with those who were uncomfortable with being touched. When I finally did attract in a relationship with someone who was equally super passionate, then that person strayed. My lack of trust in relationships did not help. The days where I was not with my partner I would assume they were up to no good since they all ended up doing that anyway. I had to drop my guard and have faith that they are not all the same way. I also had to find a way to stop attracting in the same types of characters. Anything less than compromise is unacceptable in a relationship.

My vibration had risen to a great degree in my mid to late thirties. I made a pact to not get involved with anyone who I considered less than my equal. The only exception would be if I was meant to teach them how to be in a relationship per my Spirit team's instructions. If this happens to you, then you will have to know the difference between someone willing to learn and someone who is uninterested in gaining knowledge, but instead antagonizes you. If they are not in it to learn, but criticize you, then its time to end the relationship. We are in soul mate relationships to teach and to learn from one another. I came to the conclusion that I would sacrifice myself by waiting for the right one if necessary, rather than being with anyone purely out of loneliness or the need for companionship. You can have companionships in friendships and you do not need to have it in love relationships. Sometimes we are commitment phobic for fear of being in the wrong relationship when the right one shows up. Relationships are not perfection. You are meant to work at something together and learn the nature of compromise, support and compassion. There are no relationships that are 100% perfect.

I have been around the block more times than I can count. I have had more experiences than I would care to divulge in. This does not mean that there are not those who have done far more, but I am hammering home that it was quite a bit of experience. I have been out on so many dates in my lifetime that I would never be able to tell you how many as it was off the charts. I was the serial dating King and I never asked anyone out. I figured if they wanted me bad enough, they would court and pursue me. I am not that unobtainable or difficult because I would always meet that other person more than half way. If they made the move, I graciously reached out my hand and pulled them in with me. In the end, I gained a degree from the dating school of hard knocks. Without intending to, I had mastered the art of relationships, dating and sex. This happened through my own experiences coupled with my instant knowledge on relationships delivered to me by my Spirit team.

When someone is having love troubles or questions, I am the one they contact. I soon took those teachings and began teaching it professionally through writing and books. I always found it ironic considering that my own romantic relationships were typically unsuccessful due to infidelity or instability with the other partner causing a drastic imbalance. I had to examine how and why the romantic relationships I was in were with someone who was up to no good. Add to that they were swimming in addictions such as heavy alcohol or drugs. They were experiences at that time that I do not regret, because they served a major purpose in my growth. Despite the relationships ending early, I knew that it would be good practice for me to continuously drop my walls and open myself up more to new possibilities and ways of interacting in new stronger relationships with more evolved people. Each of my partner relationships improved over the previous one. It can take years of effort to stop the cycle of attracting in dysfunctional relationships.

SOUL MATES

Everything we do, every choice and decision we make every second has an effect. This effect is what attracts circumstances and people to you. Look back on the course of your life and the decisions you made and take note at what the results were. See yourself in an objective light. This will enable you to discover what part you played in the outcome of your life and whether that invited in something good or bad. Our

Ego blames everyone else when there is no one to look at for your unhappiness, but yourself, your thoughts and moods. Sometimes we are in situations that we have no control over and are powerless, but in truth you are never powerless. You own your life and have complete control in the decisions you make daily. You may not even be aware of every tiny shred of decision making you do everyday, but you are making them regardless of your awareness of it or not. The exception is a child who is under the care of an abusive parent. When you are in the grips of someone else, stop and be still and connect to your Spirit team for the answers that will get you out of that situation. Ask them for help and intervention, then step out of the way and let them get to work on it. It's important to not just ask for assistance, but listen and tune in for the answers that are being delivered to you.

Heaven never ignores you as they are always communicating with you. If you are not hearing them, then you might be either blocked or not aware that you have heard them. Sometimes you come to find that you already knew the answer. This is confirmation that you are hearing them accurately. You were unaware that was Heaven communicating those messages you knew all along. Ask your Guides and Angels to continue to show you signs until you know for sure what it is they are relaying to you, then always say thank you. Being grateful is an important part of manifesting and reaching the life you want.

We all have more than one soul mate. You may want to meet your soul mate, but you may not be aware that you have already met several of your soul mates. Your soul mate can be a family member, an acquaintance, a business colleague, a friend or a lover. Soul mates are put in our path for the purpose of our growth. You both have something to learn from the other one that will benefit the progress of your soul. Our soul mates are not everybody we come into contact with. You will know if they are your soul mate if they challenge you in a particular way that prompts you to change in a positive way. They may get you to take a good hard look at what you need to change in your life and/ or push you to accomplish your dreams or improve yourself.

One example can be if you are lacking in self-confidence, but then an employer pushes you out onto a stage in front of an audience to give regular speeches. Those speeches change the course of your life where you gain confidence and a new career in public speaking. The union was successful in that it pushes you out of your comfort zone to conquer your fears. This colleague is your soul mate who you were meant to cross paths with at that point. The people you meet online for a shallow rendezvous or who you pick up in a bar are not to be confused with being your soul mate as they are rather a distraction delaying you from your purpose by negatively feeding a part of you that feels empty. This isn't always the case, but if you do meet someone in this way and something happens with that meeting that triggers a drastic life change in you such as permanently giving up alcohol, drugs or any other negative block or vice, then that person was sent to you for that reason. Soul mates can be the people we come into contact with for any kind of important positive connection to change or improve you. They are especially evident in the form of a friend or lover as those types of soul mates may be in your life longer than others.

You may have witnessed certain friendships that were once tight drift apart. This is because the connection was made to get you to a certain place, but then had fulfilled its mission. One of the two parties might have grown and changed spiritually in some way and the soul mate friendship achieved its purpose. That soul mate may have been brought to you to help you start a successful business and then you find that the relationship deteriorates after that. This can also be a sign that this person was a soul mate to improve you in a certain area of your life. This benefits everyone involved in a positive way and then it becomes time to disband the partnership. You take away only the lessons and love being grateful for that connection. A soul mate can be a friend who had appeared for you during a rough time when you needed it most. They offered the compassionate ear coupled with profound wisdom that helped you heal and get through it quicker. If that person was not around at that time when you needed it, then you know you would have had it much harder. This other person had the benefit of being a teacher, counselor or healer to you in some way for that particular circumstance.

Soul mate relationships are challenging in that they force you to examine yourself and hold a mirror up to your negative flaws. With soul mates, you often bring things to the relationship what the other one is lacking or missing. Every relationship you had whether good or bad was not only delivered to you for the purposes of your soul's growth, but you attracted them in through the Laws of Attraction. If you are covered in addictions you will attract someone similar or on your level. You will not attract someone who is well to do and who owns their life. Why would a spiritually minded health conscious person be with someone who falls prone to a plague of addictions on a weekly basis? If you want someone who appears as if they are on a higher caliber than you, then use that opportunity to start making long-term improvements and life changes to yourself so that your vibration will rise. You will have a bigger shot at attracting that person you are interested in for good.

My guides have shared with me that, *"50% of the people in the world cannot be in a relationship even though they ask us for one. They soon realize they don't want to be chained or tied down. They don't want to have to keep answering to them texting, calling, letting them know what they are doing and why or where. You don't do those things because you have to, you do them because you love them and you want to. You don't want them to worry up all night wondering where you are. We laugh here because many of you do not understand this today. You want it, but then when you have it, you can't do it and want out."*

We all need companionship, but I often hear many complain that it is difficult to find a suitable love partner. There are various reasons for this:

- » You are expecting unrealistic perfection.
- » Sometimes the soul mate love relationship the angels are bringing to you is being prepped and not ready for you yet. Your soul mate could be going through a transition in their life that ultimately prepares them for you and then the meeting will take place.
- » Your vibration has risen to a higher level of spiritual growth and you are repelling those you were once attracted to. Your Guides and Angels are prepping a new soul mate for you who will match that vibration.

» Your next soul mate might currently be in another relationship with someone else that your Spirit team knows will be ending eventually. They are waiting for that relationship to run its course before they orchestrate a meeting with you and that person.

» Often times a suitable companion was sent to you, but you or the other person denied you or did not act on it. Your decisions to deny it are due to Free Will. It's more or less back to the drawing board for your guides to find another potential soul mate.

» You might not be in a place where you are ready for the kind of soul mate relationship your guides want to bring you. You have your own transition and growth to take place before you are ready for a real life long love partnership.

Times have changed and half the world does not value relationships the way they once did. Many may not work at these relationships when they are in them. They are out seeking impossible perfection. They are under stress or bathed in addictions unable to attract a proper soul mate or even keep that person in their life. You have some work to do on yourself so that you are more ready for this right person. Ask yourself what you have to offer a relationship? Often many wonder what will this person do for me, but this attitude is incorrect. There needs to be giving and receiving energy being reciprocated in all relationships in order for them to stay balanced and successful.

It's taken me a long time to get into the cycle of giving and receiving. I am a natural giver and have been uncomfortable receiving and that created issues in my past relationships. When you give and overcompensate, then that creates an uneven connection. You need to give and receive which creates an ebb and flow of energy. The same goes for those that are always receptive or receiving gifts, but not giving back in any way, then that creates imbalance and blocks in the relationship. This does not just apply to relationships, but it applies to your life in general. Giving can be as simple as smiling or saying hello to a stranger in passing. It is essential that all relationships have a give and take. All relationships need to have a healthy steadiness of giving and receiving otherwise there will be imbalance. The energy needs to flow freely back and forth to have a successful relationship of any kind.

You can only attract someone good as soon as you become good. Do a thorough self-examination of yourself and be completely objective so that you can find out what you are doing that is harmful to your growth. Do you fall into a daily negative pessimistic cycle of constantly talking yourself down that you are not good enough? Where are you going to meet these potential soul mates? Are you hoping they will just show up at your front door? Are you hanging out in bars, clubs or even on those nifty little phone apps disguised as a way to meet friends, but are sexually charged for fleeting moments with no-name suspects? You will not find a put together, well rounded, secure, stable, busy professional hanging out there. This is ultimately what you need for a long term relationship. In all of those settings you will typically only meet one type of person and they are only after one thing in the end. They are typically lonely and bored souls who are looking for addictive ways to fill up own their emptiness and insecurities. They are not ready to be in a healthy, committed relationship.

Do not go diligently searching for your soul mate. They will come to you naturally at just the right time. All of the soul mates I have come into contact with whether they are friends or love relationships all came to me when I was not looking. Closeness and trust must be earned with new people instead of blindly and naively latching onto them.

When you are finally in a relationship, then the real challenge begins. When the initial attraction to your partner declines you get lazy and the Ego kicks in and wants control over the relationship. It is not the real you. The real you is when you experienced happiness as you were getting to know this new person. They reminded you of the love and joy you were initially born with. A relationship is not about having all of your needs fulfilled. It is about giving and sharing with someone else. It is about companionship and learning to love. It is about lessons and growth. You cannot enter a relationship and expect it to be successful until you are experiencing content and joy in your life first. If you are blinded into believing that some perfect person is going to sweep you off your feet and then you will experience happiness, you will be sorely disappointed. The all-encompassing love you crave is your detachment with Spirit and God's love. Another person cannot fill that void or emptiness. They do not have that kind of power to give you an impossible love. They may fill it for a brief moment, but then you will be right back where you started as your previous feelings of discontentment begin to rise again. This is why it is important to make your peace with yourself first before you date or enter a love relationship. Be content with you and the direction you are headed and then will you begin attracting in soul mates at higher levels. You will be more apt to having a successful long-term relationship that goes the distance.

TWIN FLAMES

Your twin flame is the other half of your soul. Most people do not meet their twin flame in this lifetime. Twin flames are a higher form of a soul mate. For some of us our twin flame is waiting for us on the other side. They are not sitting around idly waiting, but rather they are assisting us to manifest soul mates for us in this lifetime. If our twin flame is in the Spirit world, they do not want us going through life alone. They want us to have someone to share our journey with while were here. If your twin flame has reached a high level of spiritual growth that has surpassed yours, they will already have moved onto another dimension. You will meet them when you cross over. You will not meet your twin flame in this Earth life if you have not reached a high degree of spiritual growth. If you do happen to be in the rare category where you have grown spiritually and therefore come into contact with your twin flame in this lifetime, then you may find that it won't be easy for you both. The intensity you both have for one another are extremely deep. It's that true saying: *'I can't live with you—I can't live without you'*. There is often an age difference between yourself and your twin flame. They may be from a different state or even country entirely having varying cultural beliefs and backgrounds than yours.

The connection between yourself and your twin flame is so powerful that often one of the two of you finds it difficult to pursue a relationship with the other. The passion for that person is so great that it can make one or both of you uncomfortable. Instead they choose to date and get involved with other people that are ultimately meaningless to them. It feels easier to them to do this than pursuing the relationship with their one true twin flame for fear of getting hurt. They are unable to control the intense feelings they have for them. They cannot get hurt as they are meant to be with one another. They will continue to cross paths until they accept that it truly is destined.

While one of you is in these mini-relationships with these other people you cannot stop thinking about the one that is your twin flame. You are not aware that it is your twin flame, but your thoughts always lead right back to the person you are consistently drawn to over the years. It does not matter how much you hide it or convince yourself that you are happy with this other person. Your thoughts always wander to your twin flame, but fear stops you from making a move. When you finally do come around, you find that your twin flame has put up a wall and is inaccessible for the same reasons. You are both rarely on the same wavelength of *'let's do this'*. When you both do decide to merge you experience the kind of fireworks that last lifetime after lifetime. Because your souls were split at conception the pull to one another is unshakeable. You will continuously be drawn to one another in this and other lifetimes no matter how much you resist it. If you keep on running into or crossing paths with this person over the years and you are both experiencing a heightened intensity that never wavers, then you may have met your twin flame.

You will often find that you have strong feelings for this person over the years without it ever faltering or there can be a love, hate relationship. This is not to be confused with tempestuous, passionate relationships. You could end up getting married to someone else and find yourself unable to stop thinking about your twin flame. Years pass as you are in another relationship that ends up in divorce. During this time you continue to keep running into this twin flame denying that it's the one. If you have a reciprocated, intense attraction for someone that continues on for years, then this could likely be your twin flame. You do not reunite with your twin flame until you have improved yourself and your lifestyle. However, if your twin flame has improved themselves and their lifestyle, but you have not, then it could still be your twin flame. You were brought to them at the right moment where Spirit knew you were close enough to grasp these changes. This would prompt you to begin changing yourself in the process to match their vibration.

You must connect with God and make yourself truly whole before you are united with your twin flame in this life, the next or on the spiritual plane. This is why it is rare to meet them in this lifetime, as we are all here for the purpose of spiritual growth and to learn to love. If you reach that level rather quickly in this lifetime, then it is likely you will connect with your twin flame. You do not need to take a retreat in an Ashram to be spiritually enlightened. It is remembering who you as a soul are. It is being aware of everything around you, being a good person and having integrity. The message and theme is in every spiritual, religious or philosophical book written: *Love thy neighbor as thy self.*

You can find someone you enjoy being with, have a connection and live with them your entire lifetime in a marriage union and yet they are your soul mate and not necessarily your twin flame. It can be confusing when you first fall for someone and wonder if they are your twin flame. This is because you might experience an immediate deep attraction for someone you have just met. This does not mean it is your twin flame. You will know they are if you have the same immediate deep attraction for them in five years as if you are meeting them for the first time. The intensity never leaves with a twin flame. Going days without hearing from your twin flame starts to take its toll on you. All you think about are being in the same room with them, seeing them or even just falling into a hug, all of which is oxygen to you both. This is years after knowing them rather than weeks, which is everyone's expected behavior in the beginning of dating someone you first meet. You are not typically this intense with others or in any other relationship. This is a rare case where you find it to be unusually powerful and it continues to be so with that person.

When you find each other in this lifetime, the energy is generally too strong for one of the partners who may continuously sabotage it.

They have not reached the level of spiritual growth that you have. You are close since you've both incarnated relatively at the same time, but generally there is a large gap, which contributes to one of you not being mature enough to both evolve together just yet. When you are together you are home, but when you are away eventually your heart aches and you want to be near them again. You can certainly function and you're not bed ridden, but your thoughts keep wandering back to them. These thoughts reside in the both of you. Twin flames are not an unrequited or one sided love. It will be as if you have been waiting for this person your entire life and suddenly everything around you makes sense. In the rare case that you meet each other in this lifetime it will be kismet and magic. You will both know this is it instantly without second guessing it. You will be drawn to one another like magnets. You will both look at each other as if you have known them your entire life. You will both immediately be attracted to one another decade after decade. Your energy and aura pulls you both together indefinitely.

Reconnecting With a Past Ex

Sometimes we cannot meet another potential partner if we are still hung up on a past love or an ex who hurt us. Ask your Guides and Angels to either help you release your ex or mend the relationship if it is meant to continue in an improved way. Your Spirit team needs to know that you are absolutely ready before they can get to work on it. If you have a huge pull towards your ex that is not negative, but a lingering attraction, then there could be a couple of possible factors. You both merged together the first time prematurely and this is why it ended. One or the both of you were not quite ready to receive the relationship in the right spirit. Or one of you was rushing it before it was time while the other was moving too slow. It is not uncommon for people to re-connect with their ex only to discover that the relationship is better than it was before. They had time to live, learn, grow and mature. Another reason ex's get back together at a later date is if there were no threatening reasons for you two to split to begin with such as addictions, cheating or abuse. State clearly with your Guides and Angels to either release your ex, or if you are meant to reconnect to allow that to happen that benefits all involved. This is in keeping that you are both healed enough to forge ahead with a new relationship with one another, or dissolve your love peacefully so that you can be open to the right soul mate relationship.

I had some residual emotional damage from all of my past love relationships and this had built a wall around my heart that required a monumental effort to scale. I guard my heart carefully and with good reason. If one wants to finally have the type of relationship that you crave, you will have to let your defenses down. You will have to know the person well to be comfortable enough to do that. The person you get involved with should have an openness about him or her that will allow you to open up to them on many levels. This knowledge will help you feel safe and secure enough to trust someone new. When I went through my spiritual transformation, I had added, *"Please assist me in eliminating all these toxic, dramatic, unnecessary relationships that were only hurting me so that I will be completely free and clear to receive this great soul."* You do not want to be prevented from connecting to your soul mate because you are absolved in pain over your last one that hurt you.

I am a love addict and with that I have ended up in some serious jams in my dating life. I have found many to latch on to me like a snake to a vine as if I have opened them up in ways where no one has. I would often hear them say at some point, "I have never been able to open up to anyone the way I can with you." Naturally they would be falling in love, but I would not be in the same way. I adored them as I do all souls, but I did not experience that kinetic spark you have when you know this is a potential partner for you. I was aware of this pattern throughout my dating life. One of the main roles my guides have shared with me is that I am a love teacher. These prospects and suitors were meant to cross paths with me in order to learn how to open up their heart center Chakras. The gain I had with each of them was mainly to teach them about love while learning to accept that this is the position I am to take. They were essentially a student and whether they were older than me or younger is irrelevant as it was the same class lesson for all. Age has no relevance when it comes to Spirit and Heaven. Those restrictions and fads are what we imposed as socially acceptable or not.

THE HUMAN HEART

We must all be expressing love with one another. Be aware of how you behave towards others. I hear so many complain about what others are doing to them. They do not take any accountability for the part they played at all. Be mindful of your own faults so that you can improve yourself and your life in the process. We are not here to live carelessly and recklessly with abandon. Do not assume it is okay to treat people badly. Wake up and give yourself the occasional scrutinizing self-examination on how or where you are acting out inappropriately. Include how you are with strangers and especially those close to you. This waking up realization is in the same vain as someone who drinks heavily and one day comes to the conclusion that they want to stop. "Admitting" is the first step to recovery, because then your focus is on cleaning up your act. You hit that awareness point when you are accurately receptive in receiving clear messages from your own Guides and Angels urging you to eliminate certain people or negative behavior patterns in your life. It is your own Spirit team who has been nudging you all along, but your Ego denied it and only wanted the self-gratification to feed the emptiness within you. This is the point of higher consciousness where you are totally clear about your behavior patterns and your lifestyle. Growth takes time and does not happen over night. If you are doing the work then people who haven't seen you in years will notice the changes in you. They will know that you are not quite the same person you once were, but you are better!

Everyone has their lists of wants and needs in someone they want as a partner and yet some of them are unrealistic. The one thing rarely seen on these lists is the word 'love'. How about: *"He/She has to be able to love and give love."* They might say they have much to offer and go down the list, but few fail to say, *"I have a lot of love to give."* Why do you want to be in a relationship if you do not feel you have much love to give? I am out there in the trenches and I come face to face with the Ego in others all day long. Many of us do unless we are living in a quiet, rural or country setting where Spirits power is heavy and easily accessible. This is the term when you hear *power place* in areas such as Arizona or the desert. Wherever there is vast regions of nature and quiet will give you a good idea where to go to connect to your Spirit team.

We were born out of love and with the greatest capacity to love. Unfortunately negativity and Ego-based thoughts like judgment, hate and anger take over. All of those negative thoughts and feelings stem from deep-rooted fear. You have to have great strength to not allow yourself to be swayed by others or your own Ego. The Ego is strong and can overpower the more sensitive. The more sensitive are powerful than the Ego in the end. This is why we hear that love conquers all. People are afraid of being alone so they conform to their peers, their community and family so as not to be an outcast. They go along with false friendships, relationships and acquaintances to keep from being lonely. They mistakenly believe that if they sell out and conform, then they won't have to be worried about being lonely. Nobody knows who you truly are in that state. You have been inauthentic and are putting on a forged face. Go it alone even if it means you will be alone. Do not compromise your integrity for fear of loneliness or being misunderstood.

ASKING FOR HELP IN FINDING A SOUL MATE

Ask your Spirit team to work on bringing a specific soul mate partner to you. You can even call a band of angels that is at times referred to as the Romance Angels. They are similar to the cherub angels one might see depicted in Valentine's Day greeting cards and memorabilia. They often work as a team in three's. It does not matter who you choose to ask for assistance as your request is heard and the right spirit guide or angel to assist you in your goal will come in to help. Asking God for help with anything is the ultimate go to power for your Earthly needs, including manifesting soul mate relationships. If you are calling out to your guide or angel you are simultaneously bringing in God. You can do this the same way you ask for their intervention for anything else like mentally, out loud or in writing. I have found in the past that I would write them a letter describing the kind of soul mate I wanted, but I would neglect to be specific.

Every person I was serious with seemed to regularly hang out in the bars, the clubs or other sketchy places that the average person might question. They would meet people there and some would even go home with them or bring them home to their place. They would stray or date around and chat with other potentials while continuing to *hang* out with me. All of the people I romantically attached myself to in the past had exhibited this behavior at some point. This is what I was attracting into me. I had to take a good hard look at who I was allowing in my vicinity and to put my foot down immediately. The irony is I didn't meet any of them that way so I naturally assumed they had the same values I did.

Since we are not as objective about our own lives the way someone else might be, a block is formed and you do not pay attention to the red flags until it is too late. By the time I was in deep in these relationship scenarios, that's when I started discovering how they spent their free time. I quickly went back to my letter to my Guides and Angels and would revise it by adding something like: *"This potential partner is not someone who hangs out in the bars or the clubs and nor do they go home with these people. This is someone who is not dating around and in fact is also like me in that they are waiting for the right one before uniting with just anyone, even if it takes years."* It is important to be clear in your request, because your team may bring you the perfect soul mate, but then you discover things about them such as they are not passionate or romantic and that's a big deal to you. Or as I stated in my case, they are not out there searching and meeting other people.

You need to compromise and accept certain things about your partner. There are some things that you know you absolutely will not tolerate. The things I suggested for myself are what many people want when it comes to a soul mate. We all want a solid, healthy partnership. I would have no problem sitting in a lounge with the one I am with for a glass of wine or a beer. It is another thing if that person I am with is at the bar alone regularly or meeting new people that way. There is a fine line between both and yet it is important that I, or you, do not jump to conclusions even though what appears on the surface might be questionable.

When looking to get into a serious relationship with someone you do not want to end up with someone who is not ready for a real relationship where there is no *out*. You cannot be with someone who needs to have an escape route or who is commitment phobic. Many of us more than likely have experienced this with others we cared deeply for or we may have been that way ourselves. I can attest that I have and so have my suitors. Even though that person might tell you differently and that they just haven't met the right one. The truth is they are not ready and will find excuses to avoid settling down.

Write a letter to God, your own Spirit team of Guides and Angels pouring your heart out about what traits you are looking for in a romantic partner or friendship. Let them know what you will not be okay with. Ask them to bring you both together and to give you courage to speak to each other when you cross paths. This is important because how often do you find that you are attracted to someone who feels the way you do and yet you are both silent and afraid to say hello? Some do not realize that the one for them has been in front of them all along. This is because they might be addicted to the adrenalin rush that comes with pining over the wrong one. They may be disillusioned to believing that there is something better out there. They may still have some things to work on within themselves first before they can attract in the right person.

The stable love interest that comes into your life is actually the one that is more likely to be the one for you. They may seem nothing like you would typically be attracted to. Perhaps they might seem on the boring side or too domesticated at first. The truth is that the excitement of chasing someone who appears to be immediately electrifying is actually wrong for you. You are chasing after a mirage and therefore ultimately get burned or disappointed in the end due to their instability and ability to not commit. The less glamorous choice is generally the one that turns into a real and lasting love relationship. This isn't to say that you are settling for a life of boredom, in fact, it's the opposite with the right one. Your Spirit team knows that you might crave a certain type of relationship with one person who is loyal and disciplined and yet is also powerfully passionate in the bedroom.

I would go back to my relationship request letter to my Guides and Angels and continuously revise it. Naturally the letter grew to be a couple of pages long. I would go back after being disheartened by a suitor's behavior choices and add additional things like: *'It is mandatory that this person be loyal, loving and compassionate. They must know the value and rewards of building a slow and steady long-term relationship that has security and friendly companionship.'* I know you would think that those would be obvious traits in a partnership, but you would be surprised how often it is not. You do always want to end your letter and requests with, "This—or something better God." You do not want to limit yourself from being with someone that your Spirit Team knows you will enjoy more. I still ask that we be attracted to each other knowing that this is a given anyway. You are not going to run off with someone you are not attracted to. There is a difference between lusting over a good-looking model and someone that you have true feelings for their soul. You may also be brought someone to you who is attractive to others, but you are not attracted to them until you get to know them over time. There are endless cases where couples admit that they were not initially interested or attracted to the person they are currently in a long-term relationship with. This is real love which grows over time, whereas fleeting love is one where you are immediately into them for a couple of weeks only to die off leaving you feeling dejected. The younger you are the more likely you are attracted to something immediate that has no substance in the end. This is because you are lacking in life experience, maturity and knowledge to appreciate someone's true soul and character.

Since being passionate, romantic, giving and intimately sexy are a big deal to me, I would add that into my letter as well. I even added that I want a highly charged sex life with this one person. For me being physically touched and kissed repeatedly is oxygen to me. I have been this way my entire life and its not going to change. I am a walking love bug, which can be a handful or detrimental to my state if put in the hands of the wrong suitor who is passion-less, not romantic or loyal. This is the same endorphin releasing I get through exercise. Touch has therapeutic benefits that promote a healthy body. If you are someone who is not particularly passionate or interested in being with someone who is romantic and always touchy feely with you, then this is an important detail for you to put into that request. You do not want to have a suitor delivered to you who is always showering you with kisses only to find that it continuously gets under your skin prompting you to pull away. You both end up suffering and the relationship crumbles. Or worse is that it leads one of you to seek out what's missing in someone else. This is never advised, as you should always mend the relationship and work on it first. If all possible angles have been established and you have both come to the realization after a long time that neither of you have been happy, then dissolve the union peacefully.

When I had previously made my dramatic spiritual change and growth I had to add an extra detail to my letter that was not there before. It had to be revised so that I could request that this person be spiritual in nature or spiritually minded. This person does not have to practice it or even understand it, but this is a big part of my life. If I can't talk about it for fear of being judged, then it is not going to work with that person. If I'm with someone who attempts to continuously debate it, then I'm with the wrong person. It's safe to say or request that this person be spiritual themselves or at least be open minded, accepting and supportive of it. I am walking the talk and living as healthy of a life as I can. If find myself involved with someone who is out partying all night, then clearly I've made a mistake in who I have attracted in. However, that was my former life that attracted in those types of characters and I am no longer attracted to that. I cannot even fake interest because we are two different people with different lifestyles. I have had enough experience to know to pull out of the connection immediately if I suspect something that no longer jives with my values.

My letter and request would eventually grow into several pages long wrapped with layers of detail. I am using what I have done as an example of how trivial it might seem to someone else, but to you it is not. These are things you enjoy doing and want to be able to do them with this one person in a relationship. You are also manifesting this and attracting it to you by writing it out in a letter similar to a vision board. I would add extra colorful things to this letter such as this person must be nice, caring and stable. They are someone to relax or have fun with.

Sometimes we go out for date night once a week, while other times we are perfectly content to stay at home and watch movies entangled on the couch or on the bed together. We are developing something meaningful over time. It is someone who does not date much, but has mainly been involved in long-term relationships. This person has not had many romantic relationships or dated around. The reason for this is those who tend to date around quite a bit, or who are having several mini-relationships that only last an average of a couple of months, are more likely to be unstable and non-committal. If they had done this in an earlier part of their life as I had, then that was who they were then, but not who they are now. Those who are not dating around are careful in choosing a mate, because they take the process and that person seriously. They are investing themselves with this person and expect the same in return. They are completely ready for something real and tangible with someone else.

When I had my major spiritual transformation as I describe in my book, *"Reaching for the Warrior Within"*, I was no longer going out with anyone and everyone who showed the slightest interest. This would deem impossible anyway considering that I receive messages by the dozens regularly. I made a pact to move towards people who practiced a healthy lifestyle as well as conscious positive thinking. This eliminated about 99% of them! You can get a good grasp of the circles I was travelling in. Besides the typical wear and tear, peaks and valleys of relationships in general, I know that there will be issues every now and then in my relationship. The problems that arise with myself, and the one I'm with will be tepid. We will work through them swiftly and always make up immediately if there is a minor rift that pops up.

What I have described is an example of what you can put into this letter to your romance angels or guides. You do not want to forget the details because you would be surprised that the angels fulfill your request as you have asked. You finally meet and connect with this wonderful person who exudes the qualities you asked for, but then they display a negative trait you forgot to mention. Start bringing more love in your life today by exuding and displaying those traits yourself.

Chapter Eight

PRAYERS, AFFIRMATIONS, MANIFESTING

WE ARE IN A CRITICAL state as a human race. Many people are unhappy with where they are at in their lives reaching for a miracle or an answered prayer. You wake up in the morning and your mind immediately goes into worry or something negative. You know how this makes you feel and it's not pleasant. This is how you have set the tone and theme for your day. I have certainly had those moments in my past. Today every morning my eyes open I move into a channel and communicate with my Spirit team. I may ask them, "Is there anything I need to know right now?" and/or "Is there anything you would like to discuss?" I will also let them know where I am grateful and thankful followed by positive affirmations. Positive affirmations have a higher frequency vibration when you say them. When you say this line: *"I'm broke and never have any money."* How does that feel to you? It feels yucky doesn't it? I felt that just writing it. Well, guess what you're summoning? You're bringing in more of that *broke* stuff to you. How about instead you say something like: *"I have plenty of money. I am taken care of and my needs are met in all ways."* Notice how saying that makes you feel. Your lower self, which is the imposter self, will chime in at about this moment. *"Yeah, well I don't have a lot of money. I wish."* Or, *"I'll never get that job. I'm too old. I'm too fat. They want someone younger and better looking."* When your Ego and lower self get in there they seek to undo the greatness that you were born with. Your lower self does not want to see you happy or succeed. Your higher self knows there is plenty to go around and makes sure you are taken care of.

"I'm never going to get that job." This feels as if there is a heavy weight of an elephant sitting on you. You suddenly feel low and worthless and begin attracting that same energy in. What spirals in is a domino effect of more things that only increase those feelings of low self worth.

Now say firmly believing it, "I WILL get that job."

Much better.

Now say, "I HAVE this job and all is wonderful."

Even better!

Say it as if you have it and mean it. Even if you don't have it yet, say it as if you do every single day and never stop saying it. This is what a positive affirmation is. The three main aspects in our lives where people struggle the most are career, love and health. These are the areas that people often want to look at when they get a psychic or angel read. When you fight needlessly against the current, then your circumstances only get worse. This is due to the energy you are putting out there.

Because our souls often feel trapped in human form in this heavy and dense atmosphere, our lower self and Ego rises and becomes attracted to material and superficial things. Our souls are limited in our bodies for a reason, but the angels, guides and spirit souls are unlimited. We lose ourselves in outside events forgetting who and what we are. If you use negative affirmations, then through the law of attraction you bring more of that negativity to you. You are always manifesting whether you like it or not so you may as well manifest what you want. Use positive affirmations and words when you speak, think or write so that you can attract that same energy in. Try it out for a week and observe how things improve for you. As you will discover, this will take practice, because it isn't long before the Ego gets angry and attempts to take over once again. It doesn't matter if your Ego fights you on it, because you can train your higher self to take it right back! Always revert to seeing things as working out positively in your life in amazing ways.

We have all at one time or another experienced a situation where perhaps our work life is on cloud nine, while another part of our lives suffer such as love and relationships. It may feel like one area of your life is mastered while the other areas are lacking in positive vibes. If you excel and shine with confidence whenever you are at work, then this is a good example where it comes to you naturally. This state is a positive form of manifesting. Your lower self does not question it or think about pulling you down. This is the same as creating a vision or dream board. You are saying the magic words without realizing it. Look at how self assured you are at work. You can do it effortlessly and blissfully. This is the state where you manifest positive circumstances in other areas of your life. You have the positive visions in your head and know how to accomplish what you need to when you are at work. This is how I obtained the things I wanted in my life. I saw it in my mind beforehand, even though it would seem impossible to someone else. I didn't care. I knew and felt it in my gut and every cell of my body. I paid no mind to anything else including my lower self and I obtained what I envisioned.

Never discredit the power of prayer. I've spoken to people who do not believe in prayer as they do not believe in God or that there is a higher power. They may not pray because their prayers had never been answered before. They may suddenly call out to God when something detrimental happens to them or to someone close to them. God notices that we will often cry out for him suddenly in a panic. He wants you to always communicate with him and not only when there is a dire circumstance begging for his intervention. He will of course intervene, but wishes to have a closer relationship with you beyond needing help. Prayer has provided miracles over the centuries to millions of people. I have witnessed the marvels and wonders that have taken place by praying. It is not enough to just pray, but to keep an optimistic mindset. If you pray, but continue to fall into deeper despair, then pray for help with your emotional state. Once your emotional state is back to full power, then you are in that space where you can pray with detachment for the outcome of your desires.

Pray with intention. This is where you experience it everywhere such as your heart, stomach and mind. I have noticed great changes within and around me only after I prayed. Prayers are also positive affirmations. It does not matter how you pray or whether you recite positive affirmations. It is all the same intention and God, the angels and your guides are right next to you hearing every word. There is no wrong way to pray. Traditional religions have shown one often depicted as kneeling down by a bed with their hands clasped together while others may bow. It does not matter how or where you do it. It can be done anywhere. You can communicate with God mentally in prayer as you are walking to your car, driving or sitting at a spotlight. Of course you won't have your eyes closed and hands clasped together in those cases. The point is that it does not matter how you are doing it. Prayers are communicating to God out loud, mentally or in writing. Prayers are asking for help or thanking God and your Spirit team for their assistance. Praying is praying for other people too! You do not want to be slacking in that department either. If someone is cruel to you, it is easy to want to lash out or become negatively affected. Try praying for that person who was cruel. Request that they receive intervention and assistance to operate from their higher self. It does not matter how or where you pray, but just that you do it. I would not continue with something if there were no results.

There is often a bad rap by some atheists towards certain religions or people that pray to God. They may say something like, "How can they talk to someone in the sky who does not exist?" To them He does not exist, but to others He does. I do not blindly know that He, the Guides and Angels exist. I have experienced great things firsthand for being connected to them. I have tested them by asking for things as simple as a parking spot twenty minutes before I reach my destination and would see it happen. I am always communicating with Him daily and subsequently receiving results. It is important to remember that prayers are not always answered in the way you expect or hope. Sometimes they are answered in another way you never thought of. When it comes to God and Heaven, it is important to keep an open mind. Nothing has happened when I have not asked for it. I have mentally asked and then I watch it come true. Sometimes it is immediately and sometimes it is far off in the distance, but I never stop praying or believing. I know that there are certain things that are not happening, because there are certain pieces of the puzzle that have to come into place first. Let's say that you are wondering why the right partner has not come into your life yet. It may be that you are ready, but perhaps your love partner is in a place where they are not ready to meet you yet. They may still be involved with someone that will not last. This is why you must keep an open mind and consider all the possibilities.

Always say thank you for being helped as well. Not just "I need." The angels love it when you show gratitude and express thanks for what you do have. You do not want to become a spoiled child of God who takes and asks constantly. We are all blessed in many ways so take time out to say, "Thank you." Every morning when I'm getting ready for the day I'm communicating with my Guides and Angels. There is not a day that goes by where I am not. Some of the things I do say to them are things like: *"Thank you for my health, thank you for the place I live in, etc."* I just move down the list letting them know how grateful I am for the blessings that I do have. I feel more alive and alert when I start my sentences with, *"Thank you for...."* Those words have ferocious power. Focus on being grateful and saying thank you for what you do have and watch how much lighter and happier you start to feel. You'll find that your life starts to be less tumultuous in the process. Being grateful and saying thank you raises your vibration to the level where positive manifestation occurs.

There are atheists who have protested that they do not believe in prayer. They may however sit with their own thoughts and ponder about their life at some point. They will feel grateful for what they have, what is to come or what they would like to have. Without realizing it they are praying. They are reciting or conducting positive affirmations and prayer. It is the same concept and intent regardless of what title you use to describe it. All of these thoughts, affirmations or prayers are heard and answered by God and your Spirit team depending on what it is. Your prayers will be answered in ways that benefit your higher self. You may need to get knocked around off your high horse a bit before you can see how your prayer is indeed being answered. It may seem challenging to break out of a cycle of negative thoughts and words that so many of us use from time to time. It feels far easier for us to think and speak negative thoughts and worry. *"Oh I'll never get that job." "No one will ever love me."* How about saying something positive? Oh forget about it! Choose not to live your life in misery. Choose to live happy and grateful. Choose not to allow your lower self to have control over you dominating your thoughts and mood.

You can pray for other people and send angels to intervene with someone else, but that person has to truly want help. The angels will definitely be by their side, give love, offer assistance and nudges, but if that person is not paying attention or wanting it then there is only so much that can be done. God and the angels will stay by that person's side continuously trying to get them to notice. They do not give up on you, but do you just give up?

Here are some examples of positive affirmations:

- » "I am worthy."
- » "I have strong health."
- » "People like me."
- » "I have a wonderfully, successful career."
- » "I live in a beautiful house in the countryside."
- » "I have a loving and loyal partner."
- » "My opinion is just as valid as anyone else's."
- » "I am taken care of in all ways."

Don't short change yourself or be embarrassed as if you are not deserving of a great life. Heaven and your angels know you deserve it. They want you to be at peace so that you can fulfill your life purpose. You do not have to be on this planet to suffer. Make a list with your own positive affirmations and recite it everyday either mentally or out loud. Do it before bed or when you wake up. Keep doing it until you have obtained your dreams. God, the angels and spirituality are like vitamins. You have to keep at it daily before you begin to notice the much needed improvement and changes in your life.

Not everything will happen right away. Sometimes for certain things there are life lessons that you must go through and be enlightened about on your own before the next step is shown. If you are feeling stuck at a dead end job and nothing is moving forward, then look at the lesson that is surrounding where you are at and acknowledge this. To do this you have to be completely unbiased and remove your Ego from the equation. Look at this dead end job in a positive light and ask yourself, "What have I learned *while* I have been here?" What positive trait did you gain while being there? This is your answer to absorb and learn from. Acknowledge it so that you are open and ready for your next step.

You can write your angels anything you want in a prayer. Tell them your fears and issues and circumstances you would like to change. Remember that when you pour your heart out to them with great purpose that you are truly heard. Then release it and move on with living life graciously and positively. Have patience with the outcome. Watch the miracles and changes happen in the coming months that follow as you continue with this positive mindset.

As I stated in the previous "Twin Flames" chapter, when you pray or recite positive affirmations always try to finish it with: *'This—or something better God."* Because they may have something greater than you imagined in mind and you don't want to limit yourself. Your dreams and wishes come true, but sometimes not the way you requested. It will be in an even better way than you expected. It can be a major change or it can be subtle. Sometimes you will find you're still at the place you complained about, but then you realize that you're perfectly content there. They are keeping you somewhere for a reason and to fulfill a purpose like getting along with a colleague. The delays can be that they have much to maneuver beforehand or have a grander plan that you cannot see yet. Once again, remain optimistic and open minded to the outcome of your prayers. Know that there is a reason for everything that is happening for you in your life at any particular time. Know that you also have the power to change that simply by adjusting the way you think.

RECAP:

Ask and you shall receive. Pray about the changes you'd like to see happen in your life. Have faith and believe in it. Focus only on what you desire to see happen and not what you don't want. *"Please guide me to friendships with like minded interests, etc."* Also add in, *"Thanks."* Be grateful for what you do have. *"Thank you for keeping me healthy in all ways. I'm grateful that I have shelter, etc."* Shifting your outlook can take practice and time, but before you know it, you will start noticing the positive changes happening in your life. Ask Archangel Michael to surround you with white light protecting you from lower energies when you pray.

Chapter Nine

EMPATHY AND EMOTIONAL DETACHMENT

F YOU ARE RELYING ON your hunches and intuition and receiving accurate information, then you are *feeling* the answers. Not all communication is in a form you would recognize such as a voice (clairaudience) or in front of you like a vision (clairvoyance). Some of it is by your body feeling the answer (clairsentience). Trust these gut feelings, as they are answered prayers. Focusing on the stillness within you is where the real truth and answers are. There are some who feel every little bit of nuances around them. They may not necessarily feel the future as a clairsentient would, but they are feeling everyone's energy. Those people are called Empaths. As an empath myself, I used to self-medicate with anything and everything possible to turn it off. This included drugs, alcohol and pills. You name it and I likely did it. That didn't go over quite well as you can imagine. There are pluses to knowing what someone is going through just by having them walk past you or stand next to you. You are the one that everyone feels comfortable going to when they want to dump their problems off of themselves. This is why it is absolutely vital you take care of yourself and run your life like a strict executive. Do not be afraid to say, "No, I cannot help or listen to you right now."

Because you feel other's energies and sympathize you will have to work on being assertive in saying *no* without guilt. You need to take care of you first before you can help someone else. As an empath, you might immediately know whether or not you can possibly help someone or if you should avoid them altogether. You soak up all of that energy including the horrible stuff.

I have to shield every day before I go outside. This is by asking Archangel Michael to surround me with a permeable white light of protection. I also had to train myself to control the flow of emotional information that people outwardly direct without realizing it. If you are sensing fear, which is a common empath trait, then mentally call out to Archangel Michael to come in and extract those fears from your body. As an empath, you are more prone to being absolved in negativity and/or addictions. When this happens you can invite in entities you cannot see that feed on you. You may suddenly feel drained or reach for that addiction again. This is why as an empath you need to take excellent care of your body and your surroundings more than any other might. Treat yourself delicately and with kid gloves.

Being an empath often makes it impossible to be in crowds unless without choice like a concert for example. I typically avoid places where I know it'll be taxing on me energetically. Standing in a grocery store line can make you susceptible to soaking up the tampering energies easily. When you get home you suddenly feel the need for a nap and not know why. If a stranger is standing too close to me in a grocery store line or a friend is harboring negativity, then I can feel my energy lowering if that person is soaked in stress or any other negative emotion. They are called energy feeders because that is what they are essentially doing. They are draining you of your sensitive energy leaving you feeling worn out or agitated.

If you live in a fast paced busy city you might notice that people mostly tend to go to the store because they have to. They feel it is a drag and as an empath you can feel all of that. They typically stop on the way home from work when their stress level is in peak form. They may often be at a job they do not like or one that is cutthroat. I am currently in Los Angeles and it is busy everywhere no matter what time of day it is. Unless it is in the middle of the night, the streets are always packed. It will likely take thirty minutes to travel when it should typically take ten minutes. You are also sitting in dirty smog breathing that in along with the fumes of other people's cars. The roads were not built to handle the volume of cars that exist today. This only adds more stress to everyone's shoulders even if they do not realize it. There are things I have to do to push the energy away such as shielding. As an empath, you have to be careful that you do not absorb other people's energy or spend an immense amount of time worrying over them.

You will need to train yourself to observe "emotional detachment". If you are in the military or at the hands of someone who is or has abused you, then you likely had developed a level of emotional detachment. As an empath if you are faced with hostile energies you will react negatively in some way. You might lash out or feel completely drained. You can work on emotional detachment by breathing deeply and exhaling repeatedly until you have calmed down. Train your mind to take these incidents that come at you objectively. See the innocence and naivety in how someone else might be behaving. I utilize emotional detachment most of the time now. This might make me seem cold or aloof to someone. I pay no mind to any of that and nor do I feel guilty about it. As an empath, reaching for that place of non-guilt is where emotional detachment lives. I often hear stories or others issues regularly so it was essential for me to practice this emotional detachment.

I often ruminate wondering how to make the world and the people in it more compassionate, aware and humanitarian towards one another. I had to learn that these were opportunities for me to practice emotional detachment. It doesn't mean I don't care, but everyone is living out their own karma and learning their own lessons. It is not my job to learn those lessons or fix any of that for them. What I can do is BE loving and supportive, but emotionally detached enough that their stuff doesn't get to me and affect my life in a negative way. Emotional detachment doesn't necessarily mean that you don't allow yourself to feel anything. It means that you separate your emotions from your thinking and take the broader view of a situation to assess it without feeling it. Emotional detachment takes practice, and it's more of a learned skill than an intuitive one. I had reached a point in my life where I had acquired enough knowledge and experience with people to understand what makes them tick. My writing turned me into a master observer and this is emotional detachment in action.

Chapter Ten

SIGNS OF MESSAGES FROM HEAVEN

WHEN YOU GROW SPIRITUALLY AND transform into a warrior of light, you will find the messages from Heaven cracked wide open. I often use the information I receive from Spirit and incorporate them into whatever I'm working on. I have always received messages from my Spirit team asking me to step in and assist particular people. I tend to volunteer the information without always telling that person where I'm getting my answers. Some might get uncomfortable when they know the source. Only when I know they are open to it do I reveal where it came from or how I know something that has helped them. To connect to your Guides and Angels it's important to breathe. Take a deep breathe in, hold it for a few seconds and exhale out any negativity. Continue to do so until you are deeply relaxed. This can sometimes take anywhere from five to fifteen minutes generally and longer if needed. There is no set time frame to what works for each person. The point is that you are completely relaxed and stress free. You might be under stress and not realize that you are. The messages from Spirit reside throughout the elements of our breathing. This is why I exercise regularly because that increases oxygen that is fed into all of the cells in your body. Those cells are all telecommunication receptors with your Spirit team. Those same cells close up when you are causing damage to them through things like poor lifestyle choices, diet, addictions and negative emotional states such as anger or depression. I will often head into nature whenever I can to soothe and center my mind and mood. I have found the communication with my team to be clearer in those instances. I am always active on the go and do not sit still or relax easily. So for me to be able to calm myself for a bit to connect even deeper means that anyone can if they put in a little bit of effort. You do not have to sit Indian style in the grass by a tree. You can stroll through a park or hike into the mountains breathing all of that wonderful nature in.

Do not allow your nasty Ego to pull you under and obsess over triviality. When it takes over, you fixate over what you don't have or what you feel is lacking in your life. You panic over circumstances that are not taking off quick enough. You get upset that no one understands you. God understands you and that is all that matters. Take a step back and be of service and gratitude instead. The angels and your guides are perfectly content and blissful. Many of them including those that have crossed over become of service in some way and that brings in good vibes to everybody involved. To get to that space, close your eyes, take a few deep breaths until you are super relaxed and mentally or out loud ask, *"How may I serve?"* Allow whatever positive impressions you get that come to you be the answer. This can come to you through any of your clair communication senses such as seeing, hearing, knowing or feeling.

TRUST IN DIVINE COMMUNICATION

It took me a long time to trust anything. I did not even trust my own abilities at times. My Guides and Angels point blank said something terrifically beneficial for all of us:

> *"We want you to know that the messages you're receiving are not your imagination. You are discounting your own abilities by continuing to question your reception of input given specifically*

*to you by us, often to help others. We ask you to stop doubting
and trust more so that you can make better use of the input you
get and not question it so much."*

A solid way for you to track your own interactions with your guides is to keep a journal of the information you are receiving. Even if you think it might be your imagination write it down anyway. Keep this journal for one month. Record each message you believe you have received, whether you believe it's from your guides or your own intuition. After a month, go back to it and jot down the outcome of that message. You will be able to tell the difference between the self-generated messages and the messages received from your guides. Trust the messages you receive and do not doubt it. If you make a mistake or you end up being wrong about something, big deal, keep on going. Our Egos get in the way and create unnecessary negative self-talk that is not based in truth. Sometimes we make a mistake, but with practice you get better at focusing on what is your higher self and what is not. Anyone can connect who works at it. You have to take care of yourself on all levels as discussed in this book, such as physically, spiritually, mentally and emotionally. When you have raised your vibration on those key well-being traits, then the closer you are to receiving accurate, mind-blowing, heavenly communication.

We all connect in various ways and for me as a clairaudient it can sometimes be like tuning into a station on the radio. I can hear the static in my left ear as I'm tuning in moving the dial until I hear them clearly. This is how I heard about the 2012 United States Election trajectory and outcome over a year prior. With all of the noise in the world, I tuned that out and heard the real voices of Heaven break it down for me. They listed each of the running candidates that were dropping out in order and who would be the United States President in 2012, which later proved to be accurate. My mind then drifted off wondering what an incredible place this would be if politicians and its people were all in tune to their own Guides and Angels.

People get so caught up and obsess in the meaningless drama in and around their lives that it bewilders me. You just want to slap them away from that place. Some of the tougher spirits on the other side absolutely do that for us. It's a waste of time engaging in pettiness instead of focusing on high vibration activities. Gossip, arguing and negativity are the biggest time wasting culprits of us all. There are people who live in that state around the clock. It contributes absolutely nothing beneficial to anyone especially yourself. The energy is toxic and appears clairvoyantly like a dark, old attic filled with mud. There are stringy webs, cords and insects crawling all over this attic. This energy within that person festers and grows like mold and is a big contributor to common diseases such as Cancer, Hypertension or Diabetes. This is why you must take care of yourself in all ways and take the body you have with great earnest.

EXAMPLES OF SPIRIT INTERVENTION

I had finished cooking a light dinner one night. An hour later, I had decided to go for a walk that moved into a jog. I arrived back home and took a shower. I went into another room and checked email and returned phone calls. I suddenly felt extreme thirst, which was odd considering I had just finished drinking a huge tank of water. I turned and eyed the water bottle, but then something in me made me suddenly crave juice, which rarely ever happens. I buy juice and it sits there. I went into the kitchen in the dark and opened the fridge door and eyed the juice selection I had. I heard a hissing noise and I pulled the juice out and poured it into a cup. I put the juice container back in the fridge and heard the hissing noise again. I opened the fridge and peered in looking at the light bulb, "Is that where it's coming from?" I closed the refrigerator door and was startled on my left where the stove sits. The stove burner was still on! I quickly turned it off, "Oh my god I'm gassing the place up full of carbon monoxide!"

Had I not craved juice out of nowhere, I would not have been back into the kitchen until the next morning. That would have been another twelve hours later to find the stove still on or an explosion. Who knows what would've happened. The thirst and sudden crave for juice was prompted by my Spirit team. I was nudged to go into the kitchen in order to catch this. This may appear so insignificant and slight that someone's Ego may discredit to be pure luck. When you are fully aware and in tune you start noticing all of the little synchronicities and signs that are put in your path at the right time to help you. You do not notice these signs when you are oblivious or absorbed in your Ego.

Talk to God in prayer, mentally, out loud or in writing. I've emailed Heaven a letter sending it to myself and filing it away. I became privy to the email or journal letter writing when my father passed away. I discovered through my guides that they could read these letters. They can't actually pick up the phone and call you, but they can read your emails to them or your written words in a journal, notebook or even a book! Pour your heart out and don't mince your words. You are unable to lie anyway as your thoughts and true feelings are read and heard regardless. You might ask them for one thing, but they know what you really want.

RECEIVING MESSAGES THROUGH MULTIPLE CLAIRS

I was on the phone with a friend and I breathed in and out mentally asking to receive messages on him. I then saw purple forms and shapes coming at me. Seeing purple is common when your third eye Chakra is open. When this started happening with me I was seeing purple everywhere. I remember seeing it scattered all over they gym when I was working out, as well as greens which is the color of healing. I said to my friend, "I am being shown a red car and a guy with brown hair driving it."

My friend said, "What kind of car?"

I said hearing the word through my clairaudience, "Ford." I continued on seeing clairvoyant pictures, "The weather is sunny out, but it's cold. People are rushing around in heavy coats. There are tall buildings around and it looks like a big city. There is a subway or trolley rushing by."

He said, "I think you're talking about my brother. He has brown hair. He just bought a red Ford Focus and he's in Chicago right now. They have a train that is above ground."

I asked my friend hearing the word through clairaudience again, "Who is Michael?"

He said, "That's one of my other brother's. He's the one you saw with the car."

I said, "I don't know why they showed me him when I mentally asked about you." Then through my claircognizance and sense of knowing channel I said, "Okay, he's moving or wants to move."

My friend said, "Yeah, he's in Chicago, but has mentioned moving to San Diego, but I don't know how serious he is about that."

I said receiving probable future clairvoyant visions, "He has a girlfriend now, but she's not going. You move in with him."

He says, "What? And yeah he does have a girlfriend, but I can't stand her and I think they're going to split."

I said, "Could you move or live with your brother?" He said, "Yeah, I love my brother, but I wanted to move into his condo that he has in Chicago cause I want to move to Chicago."

Then we both said, "Hmm interesting."

There are times when just enough information is revealed, but you are not always shown the entire picture. One of the reasons is your Guides and Angels will not live your life for you. They may offer suggestions, but then it is up to you figure out what is the best course of action. If you make a mistake, then they will help you out of it if you ask them. Your life will brighten when you invite them into your house.

It is not necessarily fun when you know the person you're in a relationship with is straying. When I was twenty-nine years old, I was in a relationship with someone who was not faithful. My guides showed me the one I was with in a moving vision along with a dark figure in the background. They told me there was someone else in the picture with us. Two weeks later I discovered it was true and left the relationship.

A friend of mine called me to talk about someone they just started dating. He gloated at how this guy made him feel. He's trailing off while I took a deep breath and closed my eyes. I mentally said to my Spirit team, "Show me this guy he's talking about." I saw a guy with dark hair flash in front of me. I interrupted my friend and said, "This guy you're talking to has dark hair."

He says, "Yeah, it's black, so Kevin, then he…" He continues on not realizing I'm in a different space.

I saw the flash of a tattoo on this guy. "He has a tattoo on his arm and looks like on his back too." My friend is quiet and low. "Yeah. He has one on his arm and it wraps down his side and onto his back. Wait a minute. How do you know this?"

I just shook my head, "I'm just checking something. Go ahead."

We all have access to information about others when we take care of ourselves inside and out. Breathe, relax and tune in.

RECEIVING CLAIRCOGNIZANCE MESSAGES

I was walking past Nick, a colleague from a former job from the past. He stops me and says, "Oh hey Kevin, I want to ask you a question. What do you think of bacon Toothpaste?"

I said, "I don't know, that sounds like something someone in Iowa would invent."

He looks at me white as a ghost. "How the hell did you know that?"

I said, "I don't know."

He proceeds to inform me. "I'm talking to a friend of mine online who is in Iowa and he was just telling me that he's inventing this toothpaste with bacon in it. Okay Kevin that's weird. How did you know that?"

I just shook my head, "I—I don't know. It's just what I thought of." This is an example of claircognizance in action where you just know the accurate answers and do not know how you know. Because this is a regular occurrence for me, I never found it to be appropriate to get into a lengthy explanation with just anyone. I never see any other way of explaining how I know something. I just ignore the question or run over it with something else. As a Claircognizant I always know just how to respond.

How often have you had the answer to something you knew nothing about? You may have had that person ask you, 'How did you know that?' You stare at them blankly. "I don't know." That's a perfect example of how messages are delivered to you through your claircognizance channel.

HEARING THE RIGHT VOICES

There were times in my earlier life where I did not know if the voice suggesting things was my Spirit team or my imagination, but then it would later come true. I would wonder, "Who is talking to me?" I can be super hard on myself so that's how I am able to often tell the difference between what's me and what is a higher being communicating with me. Your Guides and Angels don't give you a hard time. You give yourself the hard time. That's your Ego. That's how I differentiate. The Ego wants to make you uncomfortable and say that you can't do anything. Spirit starts sentences with, '*you*' or '*we*', while you start sentences with, '*I*'.

For example: "**I'm** not going to take that art class because they will all discover **I** am not creative." Whereas the angels will say, "**You** will take this art class as **you** are going to be a financially, successful painter. Pay attention when we communicate with you as we have important guidance on the next step once you complete this action."

I had fallen into one of my mini-channels where Light energy began flying towards me in what appeared to be a dark portal. The lights were purple and then gold. I began hearing words from the other side. I said that I wanted to know who was around me. I heard the disembodied voice of my grandmother. I asked if she had anything she wanted to tell my mom. She said to give her lots of her love. I said, "Okay well how do I know this is you?" I received a clairvoyant vision of a sparkled image coming at me. It formed a silhouette of my mom and blue light flashes flew out of it. My Grandmother said, "She is wearing blue today."

I later phoned my mother and without telling her any of this I asked, "Were you wearing blue today?"

She said, "Yeah, I had on a blue shirt this morning and then changed into a Turquoise shirt this evening. That's a good guess, how did you know?" Those who are non-believers or skeptical of messages from Heaven may typically respond with something like, "Oh wow, what a great guess!" Or they might say, "Wow you are so bright."

Knowing that we are not alone and there are Spiritual Helpers on the other side assisting us to have a peaceful life full of abundance takes practice, faith and trust. I have off days as we all do, but I'm fully aware of those days. I pray to release the burdens that I accumulate as it comes. I have battled trying to connect with so much going on in my head that it's impossible to shut it off. I would worry whether or not I was on the right path just like anybody else. I would be working on writing pieces where I'm blocked and experiencing a blank slate, then when I'm knee deep in it I would wonder if I was making a mistake. You can see how the lower self wants to argue with your true higher self and delay you from doing anything.

IGNORING HEAVENLY MESSAGES

Sometimes reading for others or intervening to help someone does not always go beautifully. There are times where I've read for others and they refused the guidance and messages I was asked to relay.

My Guides and Angels asked me to let Lisa know that she needs to get outside more. This could be a calming locale such as a park with trees and flowers to awaken her state of mind and pull her out of isolation. They said she needed to open her windows and let fresh air in daily. She also needed to exercise more than she currently was. This much needed advice they told me was blocking her and preventing her from reaching true happiness with work and love. Her response was she can't leave her house and she doesn't have time to add in an extra day of exercise. She informed me that she is unable to open up her windows as they are boarded up. She was upset with the messages I relayed. I was shown that she would remain stagnant indefinitely unless the simple steps of progress were made. I did my part, which was to deliver the messages. How someone receives them is not my business. I deliver them and then I walk away.

The Guides and Angels relay messages that will take you from Point A to Point B. Sometimes these messages are not what you want to hear. They may advise you to stop drinking alcohol as it has prevented you from a successful career. Your Ego will see the two as not going hand in hand. Heaven knows exactly what you need to do to get to the place you are dreaming of. You have to follow their guidance if you want to reach a solution, even if the first step is asking you to clean up your diet.

I discussed this in an earlier part of this book on how they eliminated or reduced certain addictive behaviors I had. I ignored it for months, but once I was clean, they showed me my next step. This step was writing and career related.

When we refuse or opt out of following the messages and guidance our Guides and Angels are relaying to us, then we are essentially choosing a path of continued misery with no hope for a break through. The wisdom from Heaven may at times seem outlandish or impossible to follow at the time it is given, but it is important not to discredit it. They are doing this for your own benefit in assisting you with making major life changes so that you can truly be happy and at peace. Ask them for help if you are feeling fear and afraid to leave your home. Archangel Michael can assist with this. Ask them for help in finding a better doctor, which Archangel Raphael can assist with. They will not throw you to the wolves unarmed. They know the direction your life will take once you start taking active steps to improve your situation.

Life is not always easy and there are and will be turmoil and troubles that enter our vicinity even when we don't ask for it. There are other times where our decisions or lack of making a decision or choice brings us unwanted chaos. We stay in relationships longer than we should have only to discover we were with someone who was using us for superficial reasons. You spend fifteen years living with someone and only run into argument after argument and neither of you seek the help to stop the cycle or end it. You have two people in love, who are drawn to one another and should be together, but both live in fear that if they take that leap it might end badly and they'll get hurt. Avoid self-fulfilling prophecies and know that you have the power to manifest whatever it is you want.

There are countless books written about this. They all talk about the same thing. The reason they all talk about it and write books about it is because it is true. It does not matter if it is a holy, spiritual or philosophical book because the content is similar. It has been proven that someone with a positive mindset ends up achieving and fulfilling all of their dreams. Those same people that received miracles due to constant optimism can all attest to this. Someone who is stalled in negativity struggles against the choppy current growing weaker everyday. To become highly evolved and grow spiritually, you must seek to improve yourself and become a better person. Those who refuse guidance end up more stuck in the mud. If someone's Ego is too big, then they don't want to hear how they can improve themselves. They are under the delusion that there is never any need for improvement. There is always room to progress, as that is what growth is.

When you are going through a rough time retrace your steps and see how you arrived at that place. We all create and manifest our future by the decisions that we make today. If you acted naively or blindly in a previous relationship, then you welcome in the potential hidden deceit that hits you later. If you do not see those red flags, then you will bear witness to the outcome that leads you to a negative place. When you are in that state it may feel as if you will never get out of it. You are in a place with immense possibility and freedom to carve out a life on your own terms. You do not want to allow yourself to be hindered deeply in the past and marinating in anger, stress or any other negative emotion which blocks you from moving forward. You have likely known or heard of someone who is in that state. That person may be in that circumstance for decades over one incident where they felt crimes were done on their psyches. Do not allow that to stop you from finding peace and love within yourself. I had a rough tumultuous life growing up. I did not allow that to prevent me from seeking out a place where I could be fully happy going after the things I want and getting them.

This world moves fast and it is often too crowded in certain areas. Everyone needs to pull their own weight and contribute something. For many seeking out a partner in life whom you love is beneficial. This is so that you can share the journey with an immediate companion and share the expenses. You have the soul longing for companionship and you have the practical self taken care of all at the same time. Back in the late 1940's and 1950's, America in particular had crafted out a neatly organized plan where a man married a woman and went off to work to provide for her, their family and their home. The women stayed home to keep house, clean, cook and raise the kids. It wasn't long before women noticed this imbalance. They had a burning desire to head out there and contribute something beyond keeping house as well. America had a real taste of it when World War II happened. The men went to war while the some of the women took on the jobs that men would typically do. It's now essential that couples share the responsibilities. Living expenses and survival modes keep rising while work pay stays relatively the same. We're all somehow supposed to accept this greed mentality of taking from others while making them pay a higher price to receive the basic necessities of life.

Nancy stopped working after she married her second husband, Matthew. There was no reason for her to stop working and I only saw danger up ahead when she did. The job market and the economy were going to weaken after 9/11/2001 as I was shown. If one of you within the duo loses their job and is unable to find another one, you're going to have more problems than you are prepared for. You can see how making unwise decisions in the past can lead you to where you are today. There is a cause and effect to the decisions that we make on a daily basis. Everything can always be corrected once you are aware of how you played a part in it. See the steps you need to take to improve. The immediate reaction of anything that's happened to you comes from the Ego where we quickly go into blaming someone else for leading us to where we are. There is a profound saying that says being a victim is not your fault, but staying one is.

Nancy's responses to looking for a job at times would be: *'I'm too old'*, *'No one is going to hire anyone who is fat'* or *'I don't have a degree.'* The Ego makes one excuse after another to stop you from doing anything. People of all ages, looks and who don't have a High School Diploma go out there and get jobs because they have something else: Drive, persistence and passion. They are self-taught and they believe in themselves. Let your true-self shine through every interview and endeavor you undertake. The majority of the jobs I obtained had nothing to do with anything except my personality. I walked in there unqualified and untrained. I would become friends with the employer during the interview so that they would be connected to someone with a personality rather than just another face answering the same job preliminary questions. Communicate with your Spirit team and ask for their assistance with you when job hunting. I've mentioned to this to some who discredit it. They do not ask for help and therefore do not get it.

I went through periods of guilt, because although I have my own neurosis I had finally reached a place in my thirties where I was doing well, spiritually, emotionally, physically and financially. I have been taken care of in all ways since then as I paid my former Karmic debts to society. I ultimately surrendered permanently to the care of the Spirit and the Creator. I eventually became a spiritual teacher and healer living in the Light as best as I possibly can. They showed me that I lived a tough life and came out of it unscathed. I did not back down from going after what I wanted to do. I would take on everybody else's issues as the go to person. The angels had shown me that would darken and drain my energy if I did not back down. It was important to take constant breaks of me-time to re-charge. If I didn't take my time seriously, then I would grow scattered and sloppy in my connections and choices subsequently experiencing burn out. The world is changing so rapidly and many people are paralyzed with fear and anxiety about the future. The angels can guide us through these changes, and give us solid guidance that we can trust. They help us to stay calm during crises, and heal away negative situations, while extracting the lessons contained therein as well.

SPIRIT IN THE SKY

One morning I awoke and immediately went into a channel with my Guides and Angels. This is common for me as I always find it to be a great way to start the day. You are super relaxed and open to communicate. I have heard from some that the second they open their eyes they have worry on their mind. This is no way to set the tone for your day. I have been guilty of it as well in the past. Give your worries to Heaven in a mental prayer or affirmation in the morning. Whenever you are stressed or tired, then that is your body trying to tell you something. The angels urge you to pause and retreat as much as possible. They see when our souls are over stimulated and when you cannot afford to absorb any more input from the outer world. The energy of the outer world is intense everyday now, which is why it's crucial to take several time outs. On days that you are unable to, do your best to sense, feel, hear or know the voice of your higher-self coming through the noise. Even if you're not sure if you're making contact, you are. They are always responding even if you're temporarily blocked or unsure.

That morning when I awoke they asked me to turn the radio on and so I reached over and hit the "on" switch near my bed. The first few chords of the next song began, "Spirit in the Sky". I thought that was incredibly fitting and pretty humorous. They all have great laughter and senses of humor on the other side and urge us to have the same. They prepared me for the day and to remember that we're never alone. They prompted me to get a move on. Your Guides and Angels around you often communicate to you in various ways and sometimes through music! This was their way of telling me they enjoyed connecting if only briefly after I woke up. Have faith, trust and open your heart to them. Pay attention to the repetitive signs and symbols around you, as they can often be the answer you've been looking for. Remain detached and connected to your inner voice as much as possible daily. It doesn't matter that you're mentally checking out even if you have priorities to attend to. You will still get those done by keeping one foot on the ground and another listening to your higher self on the next steps you need to make. We're urged to take pause and contemplation often not only for this reason, but were clearing out all the old energy accumulated in and around us, which can often be draining. Our souls need constant rest amongst the demands of Earthly life therefore it is always okay to take regular time outs and not feel guilty.

Chapter Eleven

WHAT DOES HEAVEN SAY ABOUT HOMOSEXUALITY?

IT WOULD BE REMISS OF me to not reveal information on one of the most controversial topics that exist in present day. I did not intend to, but my Spirit team had urged me to considering that it is playing a big part in the darkness pervading the planet. Someone who does not understand another or who hates another they don't know with immense venom is a product of the Ego and fear. There are many people who want to see death against homosexuals while others attack, condemn and harass them. There are those that hide behind the words of false prophets who claim to speak the word of God. I know the word of God and have been with Him long before I had this Earthly existence. No human soul is any more special than any other. The words *'homosexual'* and *'gay'* are not in Heaven's vocabulary and therefore nor are they in mine. I will put down as best I can what God, Saint Nathaniel and my team of guides has relayed to me on this.

*Saint Nathaniel's message
interpreted by the author:*

We attribute no labels to your souls in the way that you have trained yourself to. You choose this act on your own volition of Free Will. You are all created in the likeness of His image. Things such as judgment, maltreatment and murder are what are considered a sin in the eyes of God. Homosexuality is not a sin in the way you define it. We have to use words that you are accustomed to understanding. The world is experiencing a transforming shift organized and set out by God. This shift is part of the evolution of His creation in order to bring it back to the grace and beauty intended from its inception. You are responsible for it and how you set up your own lives. The world is at a place where there is as much good as there are bad. Dark energy pervades half of this world dictated by human Ego. The other half is filled with the light of God. This is the dawn of the new age upon us. You witness this darkness in the constraints you have created such as politics, government, social media and those in power. These branches seek to interfere with others in how they live. They persist to obstruct how others choose to set up their Earthly life as a human soul.

The Light in you is growing in numbers. They are the newer Earthly souls electing to come into this Earth life to work in making significant changes to the planet and its habitat. They are what you consider the new generations of people. They are peaceful loving and in tune to their surroundings with limited Ego. They are more privy and conscious to how they and others behave with others. They are stripping away unnecessary toxic ways of living from addictions to poor behavior patterns including escapism. Many organized religions are broadening their teachings. Others are using their placement to condemn and curse certain human souls who appear differently to them. Those souls elected to arrive in ways you do not understand in order to awaken your hearts so that you may grow spiritually. This is a way to accelerate the planet as a whole in reaching a place of love and compassion. Some of you may have a tantrum or want to stop what you are afraid of. You cannot stop what God has intended.

You have had same sex marriages centuries ago during what you call the medieval times long before you made it currently an issue. These same sex marriages stopped around the 340 AD period due to the rise of Christianity and the Christian Emperor's who passed laws forbidding it. They were infused with fear and instilled this same fear into the public. Because they did not understand the true nature, they called it a crime and punishable by their own new laws that they saw fit. This was all man and Ego created, not God created or inspired. Eventually the punishment was to be burned alive in public. This is still happening in third world countries. They have carried out with hangings as if it were 400 A.D. Some of these countries continue to stone them to death by bashing them in the head with bricks. They attribute this to the Devil. What they don't see is that the real Devil is how they choose to react. Your Ego makes excuses so that you can justify causing others grief and harm.

You are witnessing the destruction towards homosexuality being reversed hundreds of years later where you have progressed becoming more compassionate and loving towards one another. You are all of God's children and loved equally. Why do you not do this my child? Why do you fret and experience so much pain and anger so? What truly offends your fragile Ego that someone has another path that is not like yours? Do not lose sight of who you and your soul truly are and will become when you have completed your Earthly life. You are not going to Hell for French kissing. You will not go to Hell if you are in a committed love relationship with someone of the same sex. There is no Hell in the way that you know it. The only Hell is the one you create for yourself. The shivers you feel are a product of living in fear and the unknown. Do not be afraid my child. The only fear that exists is the false reality your mind tricks you into believing. We understand you do not fully comprehend what Earth's existence is about. To hear this may seem like you have had the rug pulled out from underneath you. You are always safe and always will be. Some of you are reacting in ways that have been taught and trained by other human Egos. You must stop what you are doing and the way you have been thinking to date. Eliminate all of the noise of the human Egos around you and focus on the stillness within you. When you truly let go of all the burdens you carry on your soul by others, will you then see the truth of who you are dear one. The obsession that some have over homosexuality or race and religion is diverting the world from love, joy and their life purpose. You have a preoccupation over a breed of God's creation that you do not understand. Your Ego allows this to cause uproar out of fear and misguidedness.

God, the angels and Heaven see no distinction between heterosexuality and homosexuality as long as two people, two souls are in a loving, committed relationship. We are always happy to see love being observed. Your souls are attracted to one another. Your genders are irrelevant and not based in your current reality. When you leave your body, your body does not come with you. Your soul is left in tact along with its Ego. You must temper this as part of your lesson and growth. Some of you have allowed your Egos to feel uncomfortable with homosexuality. You have allowed it to control you into forming warped thoughts into your minds that it is perversion, pornography and sex. This exists regardless of the human souls attraction to one another. Two souls born of the same gender who experience similar love for one another, know God by this act. They are no different from any other soul who craves the love and partnership of another. They have elected to come into this life as a homosexual knowing that they will put up with tough lessons at the hands of newly developed souls. They know they will put up with it by those who have had their Ego guided by another.

You are all here to set up life and provide for yourself regardless of who you choose to do this with. Those that seek to condemn homosexuals often do not know others who are homosexual. The truth is that they do. Those who have an attraction to the same sex surround you. They are forced to hide their true identity for their safety or to avoid ridicule or punishment from their communities. Many use the holy book as justification to revile others after having misread and abused the text to give them license to conduct harmful acts. God does not support a justification of evil, anger or hatred even if you have decided that your holy books do. You added text to your holy books at a later date to condemn Homosexuals. These were men experiencing living in limitations and misguided by fear. It is a danger to use God as your reason for your justifications as God only sees the innocence in your soul. These men had no knowledge of homosexual relationships. They feared homosexuality and anything that appeared to be different than what they were accustomed to in their communities. What they were accustomed to was self-taught by the society they lived in. It was not and is not God's word. God's word is simple dear one. Love. Learn to love all of His creation and you shall know God. If your Ego seeks to find ways to explain why you condemn, harm and judge others then you do not know God or the Holy Spirit. You can only reach God by experiencing love, joy and peace. You can reach him by keeping your mind clear of the addictions and toxins you escape for. Do not act out aggressively towards another because they are different. This is a product of fear and not the love you were born with.

Men of the cloth and those of the like have chosen to set up and run organizations that support human laws where countries may place rules on their unholy books to harm others. These laws seek to put homosexuals behind bars and even death. They are perpetually foolish and disconnected from the Divine Creator. They are dictated by rules earlier souls of thousands of years ago claimed to be receiving from God. Yet, there was no more input from God afterwards? Did God stop communicating? He can never stop communicating child. It is you who have stopped listening. You have men donning as preachers speaking for God that you publicly assassinate the homosexuals. You have been doing this act for centuries persecuting anything or anyone who was not like you. You have done this with the Indians, the African Americans, the Asians and all of God's races. You have done with this with others who do not practice the same religion you do. You have done this with all souls who are not like you. God did not create a world where everyone is the same. You must stop allowing your Ego to control you into experiencing fear and anger because you have met someone who is not like you. Some of you will say that you love everybody. We wonder who would befriend one who disapproves of them. You misinterpret holy text. You pick and choose what suits you for your life today while ignoring the rest and giving no reasons why. God knows your actions and what you are up to. You may deceive another human soul yet you cannot cheat God. You live erroneously and savagely as if you are doing right. You are not doing good when you condemn and harm one of God's own creations.

You have Free Will laws made by God where you may set up your life however you choose. We cannot intervene unless you specifically ask for our help. If you have come into your life as a homosexual you would do well to remember your divine heritage and pray for God to assist you in making this world better for you and those around you. This will speed up the process to peace on Earth. Many homosexuals and new generations lack in faith or do not believe or buy there is a God. This is understandable considering that growing up as a human soul all they have heard and read were stories of sermons from churches or their community calling them sinful and the Devil. You are not sinful. It is your unruly Ego that is the Devil. There is no sin when it comes to love and who you choose to love. The rules apply to you as much as they do with all human souls. Treat yourself and the people around you with compassion, kindness and love. Do not choose the role of a monster. We watch over you and guide you away from a state of mind that chooses suffering. When you feel empty you reach for harmful pleasures out of hoping to fulfill a void. We do not condemn how you choose to live. We hope and urge you to do right. We cannot cease to love you.

We do not support the need for you to have several partners whether homosexual or heterosexual. This need you desire acts to temporarily fill a hollowness within you that demands carnal pleasures of the material world. You are seeking to fulfill an absence that you believe to be missing in you. This desolation that grows into loneliness is God's love you want. It is the only love that can fill you up whole and help you to remember your divine soul heritage. It is your Ego that takes over convincing you of harm. There is a distinction between two people in a loving and committed relationship forging an alliance regardless of their human genders. The discrepancy is wide when compared to a relationship that chooses to have more than one partner. This speaks to your sensual urges that are satiated by the Ego. There is a difference between a man who is in love with another man in a committed relationship and a man who is lying in bed with many different men. This same concept applies to a married or committed man or woman who lies in bed outside of his commitment with many others outside his home. There is a difference between being an upstanding hardworking soul and one who is not. We do not talk about one man and one woman. We speak to you about two souls who join together in your Earthly lifetime to express love and cherished commitment with one another. There are millions of souls who agreed to come into this lifetime as a homosexual understanding the repercussions. There are some of you who say that you were born this way when this is not technically true. You might have chosen to come into this lifetime as a homosexual. Your attraction and feelings are not chosen. As difficult or incomprehensible as this may be for some of you, the truth will be revealed to you when you are ready. This is why it is imperative to do the learning and growth work now. You do not need to wait to do it when you cross over. There is no fire and brimstone expecting you. The only judgment that you face when you cross over is your own.

There are homosexuals who feel the entire world has turned against them. Imagine what happens when you believe that you are hated. You are not hated in truth. Your Ego functions at full force when you crave attention and love seeking it out through destructive relationships, sex or any other toxic addictions. Be clear now and invite God and the Holy Spirit to fill your soul up with the love you require.

God knows what is to come on the planet. He has known the trajectory for centuries. He knows what His creation would do and how they would behave. He knew the souls he created were naïve and innocent in their anger and actions. He still loves you anyway wanting you to be at peace. He wants you to grow and learn. He does not want you carrying around these unnecessary and unhelpful burdens and emotions. You have allowed your material world you created to overpower and control you. This has weakened your communication with God. You can resurrect it and develop it back with focus, practice and study. When you do this you will discover the same truths of where you came from. You will discover how to improve your way of living.

This requires a lifestyle change some may not welcome. This new existence will be more inviting than you have come to know.

You have been abused, you smoked, drank alcohol, did drugs, slept with more people than you can remember. You never found what you were looking for, did you child? You come face to face with misery and your self-esteem plummets further into a deep abyss. You used these manufactured outlets as ways for you to quiet the noise of your Ego. They were ways to feel loved and wanted. Release the need to continue abusing your soul. Allow your world to open in ways you have always dreamed of. The unnecessary outlets of escape harm your soul, your body and yourself. You desire the almighty's love. He will give it to you no matter who you are and at no cost.

FROM THE AUTHOR

To give you an example of the brevity of what young people are going through, a sixteen year old guy writes me: *"My whole family thinks liking guys is a disease. They make me sad."*

His family does not know any better. It's not a disease. Anger and lower feelings are a disease. Some human souls are on the lower end of being an evolved spirit. This is why those chosen ones were sent to Earth in human form first to learn something before they can graduate to a higher spiritual plane. If they do not get it right or learn anything while here, they may have to come back to Earth again repeatedly until they have mastered it. You can't reason with someone who does not know any better and believes what they were taught by others. They have to figure it out for themselves or they will when they cross over. Often people are poorly influenced and advised growing up and they believe certain things are wrong without knowing anything about it.

A good Christian woman walks the talk and lives in His presence. She never judges and has a 'live and let live' attitude as long as no one is being harmed, but is exuding love. She lives in goodness. Another woman lives in His presence except she fumes with judgment and negativity. She does not live in His goodness, but the wrath of her own Ego.

Jesus absolutely does love and accept you as I've discovered through my connections with him. You have to be completely removed from both sides in order to connect to anyone in Heaven. You are not removed if your views are set. It is learned behavior or your Ego that has set these views. These same people crucified others into slavery. The same types of people are doing the same thing to the homosexuals. Do not allow your Ego to control you into thinking that these people that use Jesus' name to attack you as being accurate. They are hiding behind his name and using him so they can have an excuse to misbehave. God accepts and loves all that He has created despite what some religions teach.

Whenever you do something good or bad this is filed away in your Akashic Records. Archangel Metatron holds these records and stands near the throne of God during your judgment. All of your Guides and Angels are highly developed psychic entities that know your probable futures, your map and life purpose. They keep you heading in the right direction. You must pay attention and communicate with them so that you stay on course and do not experience anger or sadness. The Archangels are the managers of the angels with profound and powerful psychic perception. God's abilities are beyond what you can comprehend. He knows what's up ahead backwards and forwards. He knows what you are going to think before you think it. He knows how you will proceed even when he hopes you will choose wisely.

God saw the technological age that would bring everyone to connect more efficiently. You can now easily find out what someone in China is doing if you are in the United States. The Internet was created to bring people together, but it has magnified the anger and the noise. Man is flawed and has predictably abused what it is given. People follow each other and pat one another on the back when they are doing wrong. Man has such capacity for greatness, but refuses to budge. It is not God or Heaven that takes issue. It is sections of society that take issue. They are afraid to embrace all people, unless all people live as they do. When you do not understand something it is important to take the time to understand it before you can draw a conclusion. It is important to walk in your fellow man's footsteps and understand what its like to live in their shoes. I do not subscribe to traditional religions that promote low self-esteem, fear and guilt. I do believe in the power of prayer.

Growing up I continued going to Church because I enjoyed it into my teenage years. I felt secure and safe by these people who were seemingly good hearted. I was not at any Church that was screaming fiery hate words, but they were speaking of love. The reason I stopped going was because I received all I needed to. I already knew the real truth about all of us because of my communication with Spirit. I was ready to move to the next level rather quickly. I continued moving through each level as they kept my class lessons and growth accelerated. This does not mean I had it easy, but far from it.

This is a world that shakes its fist in anger, "Hang him!" This is without knowing if there is guilt or not. Even if there is guilt, it is not our place to pass down judgment or punishment. Mistakes are made in this lifetime to be corrected. Nothing has changed from the days of hanging witches that were not witches, hanging someone because of the color of their skin, feeding Christians to the Lion's because they had different belief systems, assaulting homosexuals because they want to love someone of the same sex. Human souls have much to learn and have still not grasped their purpose here, which is as Heaven has said: Love. You are asked to live with and be with those that are not like you to build up your tolerance to learn to love.

The highest reported rates of hate crimes in America are racially or anti-gay motivated, but there are some officials who do not report every crime as anti-gay motivated even when it is. We live in a country and world where there are crimes acted on another human being because of where they are from or whom they fall in love with. These are people who have to suffer because someone doesn't understand it or is uncomfortable with it. Identify the real lower self in that passage. All of the souls on this Earth are here to share it amongst one another regardless of your interests. No one owns this planet, as it is God's creation and world.

My Guides and Angels have all told me that Same Sex Marriage will one day be open and legal throughout not just the United States, but the entire world eventually. They would not tell me when, only that is in the future. They added that it would not be anything that bothers anybody. No one thinks twice about it. God allowed us to set up shop here as we see fit even if we are instilling rules that are incorrect. It is not how our souls entered this life to begin with, but was rather molded by the communities and influences others had on our souls growing up. The main reason we are all here and have agreed to be was for the purpose of love, which I will hammer down until the end of time. All of the rest of the nonsense is "the noise" as they call it.

Chapter Twelve

CONNECTING WITH THE ARCHANGELS

THE ARCHANGELS ARE POWERFUL, BENEVOLENT beings of God that are present to assist us along the right path. They are the managers of the angels and are non-denominational which means they do not belong to any religious establishment. It does not matter who you are or what your beliefs are. Like God, they are available to anyone who asks for their help. There are legions of Archangels residing in other dimensions, but I will focus on sixteen of the more popular ones and what their specialties are. Several of the Archangels have been featured in holy books where others have reported sightings or visions of them when they needed help most. There have been religious followers who I have heard say that you are not supposed to worship angels or archangels. No one is advocating that you worship or pray to the angels because all exaltation goes to God. The Archangels are gifts from God to help each of us experience love, joy and peace in our lives. In order for one to hear and communicate with God you must be completely at peace. You must be feeling and exuding joy, love and compassion. You have to be living in your higher self's state and stripped of your Ego.

God wants to communicate with us, but you do not hear God unless you are in that state of higher consciousness. This also means that those who condemn and harm others in the name of God are not communicating with God. They are instead operating from their lower self and Ego. You cannot communicate with God in a state full of blocks. These blocks have been identified all throughout this book.

The Archangels are God's gifts to us to help us reach that place where we are fully able to communicate with Him. The Archangels are his messengers who deliver God's messages and personal guidance to us. Everything the Archangels communicate are God's word. They raise our vibration so that we can indeed hear and communicate with God Himself. Although God is always communicating with us, we are not listening if we are experiencing negative feelings such as anger, stress, hate or even sadness and depression. This is why the Archangels and Angels come in to lift those unnecessary emotions we are burdening ourselves with. They assist us in diminishing our negative ways of thinking.

The Archangels names end in 'el' which means "of God". The only two exceptions are Archangel Metatron and Archangel Sandalphon who are the only two Archangels who were once man in human form.

I'm always communicating with the Archangels everyday. I correspond with them while I'm in the shower, walking to my car, driving, riding in an elevator and the list goes on. I'm calling each in as a reminder that I appreciate all that they do for me. Since they are God's arms you are communicating with God too. He wants to have a relationship with us. He wants us to always communicate with Him. It doesn't matter where or how. It is not necessary to do it in a church, but it does help to do it in a calming environment. You can communicate mentally while you're brushing your teeth, while you're driving or while you're taking a walk. It doesn't matter how or where you do it, just talk to Him.

Calling upon God, any Archangel, Angel or Spirit Guide can be done at any time and anywhere. They are all powerful and unlimited which means that they can be with anyone and everyone simultaneously. They each have specialties that they can assist you with on your journey.

They are magnificent Lights and like God they know your thoughts, feelings and desires. They show up before you have finished your sentence! You do need to specifically ask for them to help you since they cannot interfere with our Free Will. This is God's law. The only exception is if there is a life threatening moment taking place that may result in your premature death. They will appear to put a stop to it. Many around the world have witnessed and told true stories of their encounters with the Archangels.

One of the more efficient ways of connecting to any of them is by creating a soothing atmosphere and environment in a quiet room that contains soft music playing, a candle burning or the smell of incense. Breathe in deeply and exhale out any stresses or thoughts until you are fully relaxed. Call the Archangels name and pour your thoughts and heart out to them. Do not push or attempt to receive any sort of communication otherwise you will block it. Simply just "BE". Remain open while allowing whatever messages or guidance is being communicated to you through any of your clair channels *(seeing, hearing, feeling and knowing)*. You do not need to create the perfect ambiance in order to communicate with them. However, you may find it will relax you and bring you to a blissful state where your connection is made. These spirits are highly responsive to the light of a candle and a calming atmosphere.

Archangel Michael

E VERY MORNING AFTER I WAKE up, I connect to my Spirit team and I ask them to keep my thoughts aligned and positive for the day.

> *"Dear God, please surround me with a sphere of powerful, brilliant white light six feet tall all around me. Send the Archangels to protect me from all harm. I ask my Spirit Guides and Angels to guide me, guard me and keep all negative influences away from me."*

I visually see the white light shoot out from all around me followed by a jolt of positive energy. After I'm dressed and ready to go for the day, I begin by calling in some of the Archangels that I work with by name to my side. I light a small piece of Sage and smudge it around my body to clear me as I begin making my contact with the Archangels. You may develop your own way of connecting that works for you the more you do it. I take a deep breath and exhale. I call on my right hand man through all good things and bad. He is my daily protector and invincible warrior, the powerful Archangel Michael.

> *"Archangel Michael I call upon you now. I ask that you cut the cords of fear, anxiety and depression that drain my energy and vitality. I ask that you cut the cords between (name of person) and I. I ask that you cut the cords between myself and (substances/negativity)."*

I take a deep breath and exhale after each person if there is more than one. I allow Archangel Michael to cut any cords of dysfunctional attachment to myself.

> *"I ask that you surround me with your penetrable white light (protection), violet light (spiritual), rose light (allowing only the love to penetrate my aura and being)."*

Archangel Michael is one of the most powerful Archangels in the Heavens. He has been by my side everyday for a good part of my life since I invited him in. He has appeared to me visibly numerous times over the years materializing as tall as twenty and sometimes thirty feet! He can be as big or tall as he needs to be to make his presence known and get his point across. There have been some who have confused him with Jesus when he appears as sparks of light since they both have a similar golden glow. The difference is Archangel Michael has a violet glow with tinges of white and gold. Jesus appears to me with gold and white light.

Archangel Michael carries a shield and a mighty sword made out of light. This light is extremely vigorous able to cut through anything. He is a tough protector, fierce one, nightclub bouncer and bodyguard for myself and for you if you ask him to. I communicate with him every single day more than any other being. He is the loudest entity in the heavens. He's the only being I have come to know that is louder than the almighty God. One of his roles is extracting anything that shouldn't be around you whether they be living or dead. He takes his light sword to cut, remove and dissolve things like your fears or addictions. He cuts the cords and webs of your worries or other negative feelings that accumulate around your body. Someone who is clairvoyant may see the effects of your toxic emotions as cords and shades of dirty, dark, cobwebs both thick and thin in size.

Old paintings often depict Archangel Michael as a warrior wrestling a demon to the ground. The demon Devil is a metaphor and can be a negative entity, negative energy, your fears or your Ego. He cuts that stuff out only when you ask him to. If you do not ask for his help, then you stay absolved in that state. Since I had invited him to be my side permanently he has never left. I have witnessed profound life changes take place in my life thanks to him being around me. I would never continue with something where I was not experiencing positive changes. I am someone who questions and tests every hypothesis before I follow or adhere blindly.

Archangel Michael is the Archangel who often leaves feathers around. He will do this when you ask for a sign that he is around or when he wants to remind you that he is with you. Other ways he does this is by turning up the volume in his colors so that you see a vibrant display of fireworks. For me, he will usually show off when I have been discontent for a prolonged period of time. When I hear him speak or when he is warning me of danger I hear his voice loudly in my left ear. It sounds as if a man is actually standing next to me speaking to me. As someone who has been plagued with social anxiety, I have felt comfort and safe knowing that he is right there with me. He lets me know whether it is okay to proceed with anything including if someone has honest intentions or not. He has jumped in when I have had technical issues with an electronic device as well as with car problems. With both he has rectified what is broken after I have specifically asked for his assistance with it.

One Summer I had been driving around in one of my previous cars, which was a silver Volvo. It had endured a bad car accident when a driver plowed into the front of it prompting my car to smash against the sidewalk. This was long before I had asked Archangel Michael to never leave my side. My car had suffered endless car issues every couple of months for years after that accident. It was exhausting for me to be driving a car to and from work five days a week only to have to shelve out hundreds of dollars in sudden repairs on it. Volvo parts are expensive! Friends would comment on this every time my car was at the mechanic again. *"Wow it seems like your car is always having problems."* I had wanted a better car, but didn't want to waste the money or go through the hassle of the transaction.

This particular Summer in 2011, I was driving my Volvo from Hollywood to the Valley in Los Angeles. I took the infamous Laurel

Canyon Boulevard, which is this long, windy road that crosses over the Hollywood mountains to get you to the Valley on the other side. There was a ton of moving traffic as if it were rush hour, except this was a hot, weekend day in July. I arrived at the top of the hill where Laurel Canyon intersects at the Mulholland Drive stoplight. My car suddenly stalled and all the lights on the dashboard flashed with all sorts of emergency warnings saying that the transmission is out. What?! I couldn't believe it. I went into a panic and sweat dripped down my forehead. I attempted to start the car with no success. It was completely dead and I had a sea of cars all behind me with no way to get around me. I paused, took some deep breaths, shut my eyes and lowered my head. I had my hand on the keys in the ignition and I said, "Ok Archangel Michael, I can't do this anymore. I can't keep going on with this. Please help me start this car and get me out of here safely and to a trustworthy dealer in the valley now. Don't let me leave the dealer without the transaction going through effortlessly. Please get me out of here."

I took a deep breath and opened my eyes. I heard a male voice say, "Start the car." I turned on the ignition and the car started! I immediately said, "Thank you Michael!" The light turned green and it was as if no one realized I was even stuck except myself, and Archangel Michael.

Although the lights on the dashboard continued to flash with its warnings, Archangel Michael helped get me and the car safely to a dealer. Everyone at the dealership was fantastic, upbeat and friendly. We worked on my smooth transaction for a new car that the angels picked out. I say they picked it out because we had combed through the entire lot with the representative and found nothing that caught my eye. I was defeated and didn't know what to do. I didn't want to buy just any car. I heard a voice urge me to go back down a particular aisle again. I came upon the perfect car I envisioned in my mind. It was like new and affordable with only 15,000 miles on it. Even the car representative seemed stumped and commented, "Interesting. Where did this one come from?" I smiled to myself, as I knew where it came from.   The next day I walked out to my new car outside my place and there was a huge white feather sitting on the driver's side floor. I picked it up looking at it wondering where it came from. I remembered that Archangel Michael tends to leave feathers around you so you know that he is actually there and working with you.

One day that following December, I went into a channel. I called in any who wanted to communicate to come in. I fell into a deep trance and a Spirit being came in on my right slightly behind me. I noticed the dark shadow in the corner of my eye. I asked him who he was and he said he was Balthazar. I experienced a rush talking to this Spirit that I wanted to know more. As he began to speak I lost focus because I was in shock at how potent the energy was. Archangel Michael came in visibly on my left side and he rose up 15 feet tall from the ground lighting up the entire room. His right wing went around me like an arm as he stood and towered over me. It broke me out of the trance. I stood delirious watching Michael point away telling the Spirit, "Go now." I was trying to explain to Michael that it's okay. I'm fine. Then I wondered, "Who is Balthazar? And why did Archangel Michael jump in?"

Archangel Michael has made himself my protector on my journey here. He apparently did not like Balthazar's energy and blasted him with white light to see if he would stick or leave. There was a lesson for me in there and here it was: Any time you sense any entity that is not a person or other living being on the material plane approach you or any type of non-corporeal entity whatsoever, if you are not comfortable with that energy command it to go into the white light. You will know if that entity scares you or makes you nervous instantly. If so, visualize an open doorway with blindingly white light beyond it. Demand and require that the entity go into the white light. What happens next will tell you if the entity is positive or negative. This is sometimes good or evil and a question of intent. This is how one can test it out with Archangel Michael to make sure that he is not an imposter. Ask Archangel Michael to demonstrate for you by stepping through the door into the light. What you will see will astound you as Michael will become the most gorgeous light show of colors and warm light, while giving off so much loving energy as to almost overwhelm you. Archangels are like that. He'll probably laugh and then show you his colors and then laugh again. Archangel Michael isn't cocky necessarily, but he knows he's the bomb. He's similar to a tough alpha male who struts around like a male peacock showing off his feathers with a smirk.

Most of us have come across a constant complainer. This is another form of toxic energy. There may be circumstances where you find it difficult to get away from that person. It's one thing if you seek it out, but it is another if others seek you out to unleash their complaints onto you. What you want to do is create a shield around you when they start at it. As this is visualized I will mentally ask Archangel Michael to extricate them away from me, as the energy is too harsh. Once that has happened that person suddenly stops talking and wraps it up wanting to suddenly get away from me. If they don't budge and are sticking around you, then continue to get firmer with your request. I have always been amazed at how it is almost like magic the way it happens at every turn.

Because Michael is with me everyday I may notice an odd sketchy character heading towards me on the sidewalk with fixation. Right about the moment where that character hits the white light that is around me, I notice that person suddenly shifting uncomfortably and then darts away. Before Michael was with me, I would face head on towards danger or into a character you do not want to cross paths with or have to engage with. This is one of the reasons I think of Archangel Michael as my own personal security team.

Archangel Michael makes himself known and stands behind me when I'm upset. I see his wings outstretch into oblivion and then curl up and envelope me in them when I have experienced pain or depression. During my initial introduction to him when I was doing my typical questioning and asking for proof, he started dropping feathers everywhere in my path. There was one floating by itself outside my window. Another feather was floating out of nowhere past me while I was walking an hour later. If you tell that story to a skeptic they will say something like, "Well how do you know it just didn't happen to be there." It's a waste of time trying to convince someone of a reality beyond the material concrete existence they have created on Earth. It takes more than a conversation to re-train someone's mind that has been set due to their upbringing or one that is permanently closed. Your senses need to be finely tuned to have any sort of connection to the other side. If your senses are not used or you are unaware of anything besides what fits into your hands, then you will be oblivious to the wonders that exist beyond this planet.

Archangel Michael has prevented near accidents from happening with me. Every single time I get into my car for the day I always ask Archangel Michael to shield it.

"Archangel Michael, please surround my car with white light. Don't let anyone hit me and don't let me hit anyone."

There have been several occasions where other drivers were inches close to ramming into my car. They seem to skid to a stop or miss me as if a powerful Light hand places itself between our cars. My heart would suddenly pound at the close call while I mentally thank Archangel Michael profusely. Once someone backed up into my car with their car at a stop sign without realizing I was there. We all felt our cars hit, but when we looked at the damage on my car there wasn't even a scratch. The one that backed into me however had a dent. This is thanks to my daily Archangel Michael shielding.

There had been occasions where I had attracted negative entities to my light. I would clairvoyantly see cockroaches and dark insects crawling on the ceiling from the spirit world. They are attracted to dark energies and/or negativity. Call on Archangel Michael because he is a great bug extinguisher too! I can see these energies at times around other people with my peripheral vision. Other times I see them visible in front of me around someone who is heavily intoxicated, on drugs, alcohol or experiencing potent negative emotions. I see it around those who are over the top angry or depressed. Negative spirits and insects feed off of those souls like vampires feeding on you. It only makes you feel worse prompting you to reach for another drink or smoke. They get a rush pushing you to continue down that cycle. You become food and no one benefits except those ethereal insects. You and certainly the people around you in the line of that fire don't gain either. This is why we call these 'wasted emotions'. It is pointless energy being outwardly directed affecting everyone around for no purpose except to lower yours and everyone's vibration.

One Halloween night I had gone out to a major street festival in Hollywood, California with some friends. Even though I didn't dress up or drink anything there were varying energies and Spirits latching onto me. The veil to the Spirit world is the thinnest on Halloween. My light is so bright that they made a beeline to me without me realizing it in time. Before bed I finally noticed it when Archangel Michael kept me awake. He said that he was doing a necessary clearing along with his band of mercy angels. He said that it was for my greater good. I had absorbed so much bad, negative energy from others while out at the festival that there were etheric cockroaches, spiders and termites crawling around me and dripping from the walls. It was the creepiest thing I had seen seeping in from the Spirit world. They were gnawing on some of the light around me. Archangel Michael and the angels were doing a thorough hardcore cleansing and blasting these things away while re-elevating my vibration and Spirit. This is why I kept waking up in sweats even with the air condition running on a cool night. This was an incident where I didn't actually call Michael, but because he is with me regularly to begin with, he went to work on me automatically. He has already had my permanent permission to intervene as he sees fit.

One morning I had woken up about ten to fifteen minutes before my alarm was set to go off. I mentally connected to my Guides and Angels as I always do.

Archangel Michael shouted, "Get up!"

I quickly rose and sat up on the bed. I mumbled complaining, "Why do I have to get up? I have plenty of time."

When I left the house there were several delays that prevented me from reaching the office that took an extra fifteen minutes. If he had not warned me I would have been late.

Another incident, I had stopped by my sister's house one evening and felt a negative presence in her place that made me uncomfortable. I left within ten minutes. I later told her why I had to leave abruptly and suggested she Sage her place once in awhile. She didn't think anything of it until a friend of hers who is connected to Spirit walked into her place and told her the energy didn't feel right as well. My sister texted me afterwards, "How do I Sage?"

I said, "When you Sage it's called 'smudging'. Light the end of the sage stick. Smudge it all around your body and all around your place. Make sure you get the corners of your home since negative energy gets trapped in those crevices."

She added, "My friend says to open the windows when I do that."

I replied, "No. Keep them closed for at least five minutes after you've smudged. The Sage is powerful as it grabs the negative ions. You need to give it at least five minutes to do this process and then open the windows. The Sage smoke will float outside taking that negative energy with it."

She had a difficult time grasping anything beyond the physical plane. It had taken her awhile to come around enough that she later ended up going to get a psychic read from a Medium. This woman informed her that there was a female spirit presence in her house that is negative. The spirit is red. She then added, "You have a brother who knows about this and connects to spirit. Ask him about it."

My sister asked me, "What does that mean it's red?"

I said, "In this case? Aggression, rage, vengeance."

She asked, "Is it safe to sleep in my room?!"

I said, "Yes, but it's attracted to your energy. Have you been drinking, smoking or using harsh words when you speak??"

She said, "All of the above!"

I said, "It's time to re-evaluate your lifestyle choices so they are more positively aligned. Right now this spirit is attracted to your addictions and it's feeding off of that and you. Work on being more optimistic and using positive words when you speak. This means avoid complaining and ask for assistance in reducing or eliminating your cravings for these unhealthy substances and addictions. Call upon Archangel Michael and say, *'Please clear my space of negative entities and energies. Please throw a net of white light over this spirit and immediately take it to the light!'*

She naively said, "How do I do that if I can't see it?"

I explained, "You don't do it. You ask Archangel Michael to do it.

It's not your concern or worry to wrestle a negative spirit to the ground. Light the Sage as you call Archangel Michael and tell him what you need help with. You have to say the words or he can't help. As ridiculous as it might sound to you right now, you have to say the words." I had to re-iterate to her that she has to say it, as she was always skeptical when it came to Spirit. She isn't religious or spiritual and is more likened to be an atheist.

She then asked, "Is it safe to sleep in my room."

I said, "Yes, you can clear it out now if you do the steps I've relayed to you. Then you have to work on making changes to your lifestyle by making healthier choices. Use more positive words in your thoughts and when you communicate to others.

Negative spirits are attracted to darkness and the shadows in people, whether it is someone who is under constant stress, anger or depression. Any ongoing negative feeling is nourishing food to this hungry spirit. They are not in the Light. They refused to go into the Light for fear of judgment. This will not happen when you cross over of course. The light is all love, joy, happiness and peace. The Spirit doesn't know that. If someone calls out to Archangel Michael, he will escort them into the Light and out of your vicinity.

Archangel Michael is one of the most commanding beings in the Universe. During the days when I was experiencing an immense amount of life changes, which had tons of fear energy from others around, he was popping in extricating people and situations out of my path. I was in awe and just asked him to stick around full time. Nowadays there isn't much fear energy so he does not have to step in for that much, but still travels with me regularly acting as my permanent brawny security.

These were some examples of how Archangel Michael has helped me and can assist you in similar situations. Call upon Archangel Michael if you're experiencing fear anywhere in your life or need protection. Up ahead I give other examples of how I work with some of the other Archangels in ways that you can too!

Archangel Raphael

Archangel Raphael is the healing angel. He has performed miraculous assistance and remedies to those who have asked for his help. I have invited Archangel Raphael to assist those around me who have been ill or in need of healing of some kind. This can be physical, mental or emotional well-being. He has a bright emerald green light around him that emanates off his body. He uses this light to heal those who are in pain. I had a friend with a bad throat infection. I took the role of a healer and carried out a long distance reiki session. I envisioned watching Archangel Raphael pour his emerald green light into my friend's mouth and down his throat. My friend experienced great improvement the next day and every day after that until he was completely healed. Raphael's emerald green light reminds me of the Emerald City in the Wizard of Oz. It's that bright, uplifting and joyful.

After Archangel Michael has cleared and cut my daily cords in the morning, I call in my pal, Archangel Raphael.

> *"Archangel Raphael I call upon you now. I ask that you pour your emerald green light all throughout my organs and body. Please pour this light onto my mind calming my thoughts and my heart so that I can experience love. Help me to be free of toxins that have accumulated within and around my body in all ways and in all directions of time."*

Ask Archangel Raphael to pour his emerald green light in areas that need healing, help or as a preventative measure. It was Archangel Raphael who assisted me in dissolving my dependence on anti-depression and anti-anxiety medication. When I was ready, I asked him to assist me in locating healthy vitamin alternatives while guiding me to make certain lifestyle adjustment changes so that the medication was no longer necessary. This would include cutting out anyone or anything that was prompting me to run to the medication to begin with. He worked with me to remove people in my life that were draining, toxic or stuck in negativity, chronic depression and anger. It was not my job to be the dartboard or on the receiving end for other people's negative energies and issues to hit.

There were people in my life that I would find myself getting cornered or stuck on the phone with who would be tiring on my own energy. I would spend lengthy phone conversations listening to their endless train of neurosis, complaints and issues. I had enough of the one sided friendship and wanted to find a way to stop that cycle. This was whenever I was communicating with them as opposed to the occasional issue someone might have. These particular people I speak of were living in a perpetual state of drama and gloominess. Archangel Raphael taught me that it was essential that I dissolve them out of my life. He said that it did not do me any good and I was not helping by enabling them either. They were not bad people or doing it intentionally. There was nothing positive or beneficial to have that constant negative energy around. They were takers and I was given the go ahead to add them to the axe list. Archangel Raphael worked on the list with me as this process took anywhere from a few weeks to several months. I cut out roughly three to four hundred people off my personal social networking page that I had never heard of and nor communicated with over the years. No one should have that many people on their network page unless they are promoting a product. If you are promoting a product or service, then you need to set up a group/fan page for that. I've allowed people to subscribe to my personal page, but I deny requests unless I know them personally.

Doing that cleanse during my spiritual transformation specifically was empowering and freeing in all ways as I cut out all that unnecessary fat in my life so that it was more manageable and maintained. The majority of people today seem to rely on social networking as their means of a social life. It is a false reality because people only have a handful of close friends they actually know in person. It does not matter if they are a celebrity or the President. In the end the truly close ones they have in their life can be counted on their own hands. If you have more people on your social networking page that you do not know, than you do know, then you have created an imbalance in your world. Everything and everyone is all energy and has a cause and effect. If your world is lopsided, then you are going to bring more of that unevenness into you. It's another form of an addiction as it feeds your boredom or loneliness blocking you from obtaining your dreams.

Since Archangel Raphael is the go to healing angel, he can also help you get your physical body in to shape. You can ask him to motivate you to exercise. I don't need much inspiration to work out, because I love being physically active. It is like oxygen to me. I have always been into health and nutrition since I was a teenager, yet there were moments after a long day at work of being sedentary where I would ask Archangel Raphael to give me that extra push to go for a jog or hike. I ask Raphael to guide me to the right form of exercises for my body and to keep it strong and healthy in all ways. Being physically active is one of the most important activities I love to do. I am not good with sitting still unless I have something important to accomplish. I want to run, jump and climb over everything. When I'm this active I do not crave unhealthy substances like bad foods or even an alcoholic drink. I'm way too happy and that other stuff only brings that natural high down.

Archangel Raphael can pour his healing emerald green light anywhere from places like your prostate if you are a man to your uterus if you are a woman, keeping it functional and healthy. Ask him to pour his emerald green light over all of your organs washing them with his energy. The power of the mind and working with Archangel Raphael can benefit your health in ways you have never imagined. I have witnessed his miracles in action by working with him for myself and for others. I have asked him to guide me to a stress free lifestyle and keep my energy up when I am lagging. I ask him to guide me to the right natural products that can assist in this. He always leads me to just what I was looking for not long afterwards.

If I have had a beer with a friend, then I ask Archangel Raphael to clear me afterwards. When I moved into my late twenties, my cravings for alcohol were sporadic and in moderation anyway. The majority of the time I do not crave alcohol or unhealthy foods and nor do I have a sweet tooth. You can put out a buffet of cakes, cookies and desserts and I am unaffected. I have no desire for it while others around me typically cry out in pleasure towards it. He can help you reduce those cravings and needs for alcohol or sweets, both of which are covering up an emotional need in you for something else.

Archangel Raphael has a graceful, upbeat energy and I always see him smiling and glowing with joy. This is no surprise considering that he wants us all to be clear minded, always laughing and enjoying ourselves. When you are happy and filled with joy and love, then you attract and manifest brighter circumstances to you. You are able to accomplish your tasks and life purpose with amazing gusto. Raphael pushes us to get outside, get fresh air and sunshine. All of this has positive benefits to your overall health and well-being. During the dark winter months, he'll guide you to the right indoor lighting lamps. He asks that you all open your windows everyday at some point to allow the fresh air to run through your home clearing out any toxins and negative energy that has been built up. This is something you should do daily. When it is cold you should still open your windows if even for ten minutes to clear the accumulated pollutants and energy out.

You can connect to the to the Archangels, your Guides and Angels anywhere, but the connection is heightened when you are outside in the stillness of nature. This calms you allowing you to hear, see, feel and know the accurate messages coming through from your Spirit team. Archangel Raphael is a major advocate for pushing you to get fresh air and exercise as that is an immediate way to balance your Chakras and raise your vibration level. Your Chakras are energy spots located in specific areas throughout your body. When your Chakras and vibration are at optimum levels you are happier with more energy. Sometimes the messages he gives you will be to change your diet, give up cigarettes or go outside.

Please do this often: Take a walk in nature, or through a park, the beach, the mountains or desert. Nature is filled with angels and environmental spirits around every blade of grass, rose and tree loving it to life. They take care of God's creation, as you should be too. Your own angels, God and Archangel Raphael will pour this light into your body prompting you to feel alive if you ask. Do you ever notice that when you walk through a nature setting the stresses of the day suddenly lighten or evaporate? As you breathe in the flowers and the fresh air deeply your Spirit is livened up. It's important to get out in nature and fresh air as much as possible. If you are at work, then at lunchtime or during a break, instead of eating at your desk, which I never advise because everything can wait, go outside and take a walk around. Head to a quiet area with trees and grass to regroup and realign your thoughts. Avoid the crowds as much as you can. You will notice your circumstances and overall well-being shifting for the better. You will have more energy to complete your work for the rest of the day too! When you leave work at the end of your shift, you will still feel energetic and not worn out. This state can be achieved by making these necessary lifestyle adjustments to your routine.

I have always been drawn to nature since I was kid and felt more at peace being active in a calm, beautiful setting. Archangel Raphael showed me images of the way it used to be in history and how others functioned. People were always outside in nature and in tune to their inner selves, the Spirit world and in Heaven. Before electricity existed they relied on the sun to know when it was time to go inside and head to bed. They went to bed at decent hours and woke up around the same time at sunrise. They had full days to be productive and get outside. There was a sense of real community and people rarely consumed themselves with timewasters the way we do now. Raphael explained that computers and the Internet are great inventions and have assisted us in connecting the world to one another, but that it is also severely misused in numerous ways. The flip side is that some of us get attached to it and lose our identities in it. As much as it was created to connect us all, many people are not connecting to anybody and instead constantly looking for the next best thing, which does not exist. So many people live in a false reality feeling truly alone. They want to be important and look for validation from others. The media has force fed this hollowness that this is the way to be loved. This deception exists with those that you believe have it all. The only way to have it all and feel truly loved is by knowing who your soul is. You are loved whole by God around the clock and free of charge.

There was one occasion when I was jogging through the streets and on my way home I felt strain near my ankle. I walked it off a bit and then started to jog lightly again. I felt this sharp pain in my ankle hit me each time my foot landed on the pavement. I limped and felt the sting of the pain in my ankle every time I moved it. I had quite a ways to go before I reached my destination and I wondered, "How am I going to get back on foot? I have too far to go." I heard a voice reminding me, "Ask for help!" I called Archangel Raphael and he came rushing in and asked me to stop walking. He instructed me to rub my hands together. As I did that I noticed sparks of emerald green light emanating between them. He guided me with instructions asking me to hover my hand over the pain on my foot without touching it. I saw emerald green light rush out of my hand into my foot. I thought, "Well I'll be." I put my foot back down and started to walk feeling no more pain. I lightly jogged building up steam again. I was soon jogging my typical speed with no more discomfort. It was gone completely and because I asked for assistance. I haven't had an incident like that since.

Archangel Raphael is the physical fitness angel too. Ask him to strengthen your body inside and out. By asking him to strengthen your body, he will motivate you to take better care of yourself through exercising. He will guide you to the right foods and supplements that will benefit your overall well-being so that your inner self is strengthened and upbeat. He will prompt you to lose your cravings for the addictions you are always reaching for. Taking care of your inner and outer body are your first steps in finding happiness and conquering your desires. Your life will go nowhere if you sit on the couch all day drinking beer, flipping the channels on your television or chatting online with strangers. Your life will go nowhere if you do not get up and move around and watch what you are ingesting into your body. Your life will go nowhere if you are consuming endless addictions, time wasters and around people who only lower your vibration. Believe in yourself and take care of all parts of you and your life. You have one body and one life here. Ask Archangel Raphael to work with you daily in making positive lifestyle adjustments.

Archangel Raphael can assist you in ensuring that when you travel it is a smooth one. This travelling can be anything from walking, jogging, flying, riding a train or even taking a road trip.

> *"Archangel Raphael please help me to get to work on time and have a parking space available when I get there."*

If I know that I'm going to the gym after work, I will give him at least fifteen to twenty minutes ahead of time to ask that a parking spot be available for me. I will ask him to keep the gym as empty as possible or get me on the machines that are beneficial for my body. If I'm taking a road trip I will let him know that I'm driving to the desert tomorrow.

> *"Please ensure that there is as little traffic as possible and help me to get to and from my destination safely."*

If I'm going out to eat I will ask him to guide me to the right restaurant with little to no wait. Often I would find that when I have asked for his help in things like this, that there would be no traffic at all and that the trip is smooth and peaceful. I would also be guided to a restaurant that has no wait. The days I would forget to ask or I am disconnected, I would be met with insane traffic and find one thing after another going wrong.

While I have Archangel Michael surrounding my car with white light for protection, I ask Archangel Raphael to make my trips smooth and as traffic and hassle free as possible. The days I had forgot to ask for a parking spot or even a table at a restaurant I would find that I would be circling forever with no luck. I was floored when I started seeing immediate results after requesting the assistance of these and some of the other Archangels. If this seems absurd to you, don't knock it until you try it. Give it a week testing it out. Watch what happens when you do ask for help and when you do not. You will start to notice a difference.

I miss the days when bookstores were all over the city. Now that most everything is found on the Internet, the majority of those stores have closed up shop due to huge drops in sales unable to make the rent. This includes regular big chain bookstores, which normally do not carry all products anyway. I would always end up having to order it online. The other stores that closed up were independent specialty shops that were of the spiritual variety. It was always calming to go into those particular stores feeling the good vibes in them wandering down the aisles and absorbing the book titles. I'd take down books on any topics that resonated for me and to open up my worldview. I was in one of those bookstores months before it closed down. I tripped over a wooden step and stumbled bumping into one of the bookshelves. A book fell off the shelf and hit the floor. I leaned down to pick it up and put it back on the shelf, but I noticed the title was on a topic I had been thinking about the week before. I thought, "That's strange. I don't need a brick wall to fall on me to take a hint." So I bought it. Archangel Raphael is the Archangel that will drop a book you need to read in your path or anything that benefits your overall self. This is what he does when he is trying to get your attention. Never discredit divinely orchestrated events that happen in your life.

Archangel Raphael is a powerful being that I am grateful to have in my life daily. Archangel Raphael can help you with things like: diet, nutrition, exercise, addictions, anxiety/depression disorders, eating disorders, health and even finding a great doctor or parking space. He can help you find that perfect car or home. All you need to do is ask him for his help and to show you signs of his healing guidance and messages.

Archangel Gabriel

ARCHANGEL GABRIEL IS THE MESSENGER angel who works closely with writers, teachers, messengers and speakers of all kinds. Archangel Gabriel is front and center with me guiding me as a teacher, communicator, writer and messenger in this lifetime. When I was born, the planet Saturn was moving through the sign of Gemini in my 10th House of Career, Social Status and Ambitions. The 10th House is where one looks in the birth chart to see what kind of career they should aim for. Gemini is the sign of communication so it is no surprise that I ended up naturally heading to a vocation as a writer, teacher and communicator.

Archangel Gabriel is there for you if you need help speaking your truth even if others disagree. This truth is not in anyway used to hurt others vindictively, but to spread positive messages that assist and guide others. Archangel Gabriel is the mother of all mothers' next to Mother Mary. She is there for all children protecting and taking care of them. She will step in and help someone conceive or even adopt a child if they ask. If you are having issues or discord with your own child, then ask Archangel Gabriel for intervention and help. She can assist you in creating a calming and peaceful atmosphere to raise your child.

My experience with Archangel Gabriel began in the Summer of 2011 when I began calling upon this magnificent Archangel for assistance with my writing work. I write as an outlet for creative expression, to help others, for the sake of release and because I love telling stories. Archangel Gabriel pushes me to sit down and write when I am procrastinating or staring at a blank page. I asked Archangel

Gabriel to manage my writing work and career. The first week I asked for her help changed everything for me. I had a new found enthusiasm to dust off my previous books and revamp them. She helped me take control over my career and re-ignited my passion for it. The ideas began overflowing in me and they have not stopped since. My work continues to improve and I now love what I do. Before I had asked for her help, I had lost interest in my lifelong hobby and instead focused on time wasters. I would procrastinate to no end making excuses. I'll get to it when I have more time. I'll do it when I get over this relationship break up. I would make one excuse after another. As soon as I said the words and requested her help with great intent, the changes shifted immediately. She has also helped me to speak up in my own life more that I had ever done before. I owe it to Archangel Gabriel for being my own personal author's Agent. If you are a spiritual messenger, she will open every door imaginable to help you get the message out there.

I talk about Archangel Gabriel as if she is female. I know there have been books and others where they have referred to the Archangel Gabriel as male. The Archangels are genderless and have no anatomy, however due to the nature of some of their specialties they may often have more of a masculine or feminine quality to them. Archangel Michael exudes typical male dominating qualities, which is why he appears as a male. Archangel Gabriel has a softer feminine aura about her, which is the reason that some see her as female. The genders of anyone in the end do not matter. What does matter is your light and how you allow it to shine. Archangel Gabriel has been mentioned throughout various religious and holy texts. It has been reported that she announced to Mother Mary of her impending birth of Jesus.

Call upon Archangel Gabriel if you are afraid or hesitant to speaking up and owning your life. If you are in the creative arts such as acting, singing, painting, photography or writing, then you will want Archangel Gabriel to be the overseer and manager of your talents. Ask her to open doors of opportunity for you in the realm of your gifts. If you are a struggling actor, she may guide you to a class or film festival where someone important hires you. If you are a photographer, then ask her to guide you and open doors to starting up your own successful studio.

Whenever you are lacking in motivation in your life, then Archangel Gabriel can help. Anything having to do with Children you will want Archangel Gabriel to come in assist or intervene with. She is often seen carrying a copper colored trumpet that is so bright that the light around her is a magnificent copper and gold color. Visualize Archangel Gabriel showering this light over all of your creative pursuits and your Children.

Archangel Uriel

As a Claircognizant I often know things that are coming before they happen and do not know how I know. This is a sense of knowing the accurate answers you need to know about yourself or someone else. I receive this knowledge and information from an unidentifiable source in the Universe. From as early as I can remember I would say things that would later happen. Others would say, "How did you know that?" My response was and has always been, "I don't know. I just knew." Those close to me are never surprised and just expect it. I am often turned to for wisdom and guidance because of this sense of knowing what someone should do or the answer they need to hear. It later proves to be the right decision for them to have made. Archangel Uriel is consistently around me playing a big part in relaying this information to me.

Archangel Uriel works with me on a daily basis guiding the way for me, giving me advice, suggestions and filling my mind with ideas and words. The way Uriel works is he infuses me with spiritual loving ideas where I'm able to incorporate and thread them into my work, for myself or to give to those who need guidance. The readers of my books may never know what hit them, but perhaps it makes them pay attention and see things in a greater way. The positive notes I receive from readers tell me about how they would read a line I have written and picked up on the hidden truth underneath that made them think.

I had taken a long break with writing books and instead wrote in journals and blogs. I would even consider emailing a form of writing. When I email I can often be long winded which is the mark of a writer and communicator through words and teachings. Luckily, my friends have expressed that they love my lengthy notes. I was writing everywhere except in books. Archangel Uriel wanted me to get back on that wagon again as he urgently wanted me to incorporate these messages for particular audiences. He was nudging me for quite some time trying to get me excited about it. I ignored it to a degree, but would make excuses. "I guess so. Ok I will do it soon. I know the time is coming."

While Archangel Gabriel is the CEO of my creative life pushing me to not delay my purpose, it is Archangel Uriel who is the hands on Archangel through and during the creative idea and writing process. Archangel Uriel made it so that I could no longer temper the creative juices that were flowing within me. I made the deal with him officially asking him for intervention. *"Archangel Uriel. I am ready now. Please show me the way."* It was within days of my asking him for help that the ideas began to flow the way water flows when it breaks through a dam. It gushed into my mind with mighty force. This was how I suddenly wrote and published several books back to back in under a year. I could not and have not been able to stop.

I like to use the Michael Jackson, "Billie Jean" music video analogy as an example of how Archangel Uriel works. In the music video, Michael Jackson is dancing on the streets and every step he hits lights up including the one in front of him. This is the way Archangel Uriel is with everything in my life.

He played a huge part in the development and creation of my horror drama book, *"Paint the Silence"*. I had explained to him the tone in the story I was going for, but that I had no idea what to do with it. He said that he would help by showing me each scene only after I have completed the previous scene. As I wrote one scene he would immediately start showing me what would happen next and so forth. Blown away by this process, I had no idea what was going to happen until I closed the scene out. As I would reach the end of the scene, the image popped up for the next scene of what was going to happen. He would wait to give me the next cue until I had completed the previous cue. I wrote the first draft of the story in under a month, which is a record for me. Before that, the idea sat on a shelf for several years and I almost trashed it altogether. He understood the nature of the book as I am not just a communicator and healer, but I am also an entertainer. I enjoy entertaining people and bringing joy with my stories. He said that he would help by giving me messages and ideas about humanity that were to be woven into my work. This made the message and the story meaningful. This is an example of how Archangel Uriel can work with you in most any part of your life. He infuses you with a sudden light bulb idea that benefits you and your life in a positive way. He will then show you what to do with it.

When Archangel Uriel is working next to me I experience a blasting surge of happiness as if I am on top of the world. It is the most uplifting and alive sensation conceivable. Imagine being so in love and excited about something and multiply that by a hundred thousand. Sometimes the feeling is a few minutes long and other times it goes on for hours! This is when I am my happiest and highest creatively open self. I get an overload of urgent information that I am to do something with at some point. He gave me confidence in my abilities.

For a long time I had made excuses that I was not good enough so I would hide instead or not bother at all. With him, I never doubt that anymore. I allow his words and ideas to seep into my consciousness. I bring it all out to the forefront instead of keeping it bottled up. He works with me as a thinker and writer beyond what some of us don't see or know. My existence revolves around communicating and I often get scattered or overloaded in the process. He quickly diffuses that and allows me to reach a place of calm so I can easily know what my next step is. Archangel Uriel can unclutter your thoughts and help you focus if you ask him. He is great for students and thinkers alike.

He carries a lantern or light, which he uses to light the path for you when it seems unclear or dark. Ask him to light the steps you need to take to reach where you need to be in your life. If you are a claircognizant, then you would benefit to work with Archangel Uriel. He will shine light on the dark caverns of your mind and world. If you are experiencing anxiety and clouded by judgment, then ask Archangel

Uriel to blast that negativity out of your mind so that you can see the truth. Are you a student or someone who has been having difficulty with a test or solving a problem? Call on Archangel Uriel to be your guide. Allow his lantern to shine and blast away all the debris in your mind so that you are thinking clearly.

Archangel Nathaniel

ARCHANGEL NATHANIEL IS ENORMOUSLY PASSIONATE, intense and fiery. He is ironically a lot like my personality! There is a lot of heat and red around him when he shows up. He is like an assertive, no-nonsense bulldozer. He slaps circumstances, people and lower selves out of the way without so much as a warning. He is tough and strong like Archangel Michael. He appears brawny and muscular in a similar way. Whereas Archangel Michael is a great protector, Archangel Nathaniel is more brutal in that he pushes you beyond comprehensible measures. It's not cruel, but for some new to working with him it might come off like that. You may find people you were attached to being pushed away. There is a reason he does this. He is clearing your path of anything or anyone that he feels is preventing you from conquering your life purpose. The people he is extricating out of your life are found to be toxic holding no purpose for you. All they are doing are delaying you while leading you down the wrong path. If you are unprepared for the way that he works, then it might almost seem ruthless or cutthroat. You have to remind yourself that it is for your higher good. What is coming for you afterwards will be even grander than you ever dreamed. He is helping you get there quickly by bouncing these people and toxic vices out of the way.

I had summoned Archangel Nathaniel not realizing I had done so during my spiritual transformation. Things were already happening and changing in my life and then he told me who he was. I didn't know there was an Archangel named Nathaniel until then. When you invite him in, he literally clears the decks and people will go away, situations will go away and things that do not serve your life purpose will fade away. Suddenly people will stop calling and you might wonder, "Hmm did I do something?" No. He's removing them whether you like it or not. If he feels they are not in line with your purpose and the higher path you are headed down, then he removes them and does it with great veracity. He is one tough light. He does not mince words or his actions at all. This can make him seem quite harsh and forceful in the way that he works. Know that he is all good, but just direct in his approach. He was one of the main Archangels that pushed me out towards my writing career purpose with ferocious veracity. He lit that fire in me and I have not been able to slow down or stop. I have had projects on top of one another and ideas that do not stop.

I had found it ironic that the regulars around me daily have been Archangel Michael and Archangel Nathaniel. They are both bros hand in hand working together for me dude. When you have them working together in your house there is no stopping them. You have to be strong enough to realize you will have some losses and things will fade away when Archangel Nathaniel is at the helms. You have to be mentally and emotionally at the point where you can have that happen before you ask for his help. There is generally a period you reach where your vision or your direction shifts a bit and this can take about a year to re-direct that ship. It's like turning around a big freight liner down a new course as you are making an agreement and a pact with the Universe that the time for change is now. There is a sense of urgency in you where nothing is going to stop you from achieving your dreams. In that process, Archangel Nathaniel is sweeping things, people and circumstances out of the way. It's like the planet Pluto energy to a degree where the Pluto energy tends to wipe the slate clean forcing you to suddenly make drastic changes in your life. Pluto can have an influence on you suddenly losing your job or some other devastation. The reason becomes clearer afterwards when you suddenly obtain an even better job where you are much happier. The way Archangel Nathaniel works is quite similar in that he's wiping your slate clean and getting rid of things you shouldn't be doing as well as people who are no good for you whatsoever.

Archangel Nathaniel's work has always been invited and welcoming to me. I haven't minded the abrupt changes, but rather have been up to the task and right there moving along with him. He is quite empowering in the way that he's shifted my mind and outlook to be receptive to the way he works. I can handle that kind of intensity as if it were second nature.

Call on Archangel Nathaniel if you need assistance with your life purpose, but be prepared for the often drastic changes that happen in your life. That process can take about a year or so depending on you and your progress. It may be met with some unhappiness as he removes people and circumstances you were used to. Remember that this is happening for your own good. What follows this are grander events in your life. You will be much happier when the process is complete wondering why you were so attached to it at all to begin with.

Archangel Jophiel

ARCHANGEL JOPHIEL IS THE BEAUTY angel. She helps you with the rigid stubborn stuff you have a difficult time letting go of. If you are agitated, unhappy or your self-esteem has plummeted, Archangel Jophiel is an excellent Archangel to call on. When I need assistance from her I may say something like, *"Please elevate my spirit to the level of joy, the highest vibration."*

She raises your thoughts to a more positive and up beat way of thinking. I watch and feel her pour her rose light energy over me and all through my surroundings. She will restore everything around you making it all beautiful with this light from your home, your career, your words, and your body inside and out. She can even get you dressed! If you are going on a date or on a job interview, mentally call on her to help you look good and radiate that attraction inside and out. She will spark your inner light allowing it to shine attractively.

I've heard some call Archangel Jophiel the Feng Shui angel. She can certainly help your home get organized by clearing out the clutter in your home and in all areas of your life. She can help with any unforgiveness you have in your heart so that you experience profound love and joy. When you want more enjoyment in your life ask her to assist you with that. Is someone firing cruel words of hate or intolerance around you? Ask Archangel Jophiel to intervene and beautify their words. If your life purpose is surrounding endeavors such as the fashion industry, esthetician work or interior decorating then you want to ask Archangel Jophiel to be your right hand sister. Ask her to make your work beautiful and striking whatever that may be. She is the angel that can help bring you more happy times in your life. Allow her to uplift your vibration and thoughts to joy and optimism.

Archangel Raziel

ARCHANGEL RAZIEL IS WHAT I see in appearance as a Merlin type wizard with large gorgeous wings. He is the magician and sorcerer angel since he helps you manifest your dreams as if like magic. He assists you by prompting you to go after your dreams. He will reveal the wonders on your path that will help you turn them into a reality. He infuses electrical rainbow colored lights from his hands, which he places over your crown Chakra to clear and open up your spiritual sight if it has become muddy or weighted down.

Archangel Raziel is immensely superb in working with if you are doing intuitive and spiritual work. He will bring all of that effort into fruition. He downloads guidance into your dreams which contain the answers to assist you in manifesting your desires. He holds a book of magic, which contains the universes secrets that he will pour into your soul. He's passed this onto Adam after he and Eve were expelled from Eden. He gave it to Noah so he could build his ark. Enoch received the book before his ascension and transformation into Archangel Metatron. He can help you take a leap of faith in your life if you ask him to work with you.

When you are clairvoyantly seeing rainbow colored lights you can be sure Archangel Raziel is there. Archangel Raziel has been around me since my spiritual growth and gifts kicked into higher gear. This was after I rid myself of addictions, toxins and negative people. Once I was on the clear and healthier path, then Archangel Raziel appeared to me for the next step. He comes in strongly for me, because I use a lot of my intuitive gifts for my writing projects. I write from the Spirit, not so much as the Soul. It's from Spirit and divinely guided. I write things down in a journal before I commit them to paper. He has said that I write about what I want, whereas I am envisioning what I want through the writing. If it's a fictional piece, then I am writing my intentions of what I want, but it's actually something that will sell too. He says that I write my dreams in books and then sell them. I envision what I want and I do it through the creative process. Then in my life I find that I am manifesting a lot of what I am creating and writing. This I have found to be true. He is one of the manifesting angels after all. Like a magician and like magic, he can help you turn your dreams into a reality. Envision with him what it is that you want to see happen in your life and then step out of the way so he can get to work on it.

Archangel Raziel taught me to recognize that I have the commodity here and this is my god given gift. My intentions have manifested me to where I am at. I'm using my gifts as directed from God, the Divine and my Angels. Call on Archangel Raziel to assist you in opening up your clairvoyance and spiritual gifts and watch your manifestations take flight. These gifts contain the answers to bring your manifestations to flight with the help of Archangel Raziel.

Archangel Ariel

ARCHANGEL ARIEL HEALS ANIMALS, OUR planet and all wildlife, but I call upon her to give me courage, confidence and a fighting nature. I ask for her assistance in helping me reap what I sow. She can help you in manifesting your material and physical needs. Visualize big with Archangel Ariel such as working in the career of your dreams. Envision the home you have always wanted to have. In a sense, she works similarly to Archangel Raziel, although they are quite different. Archangel Raziel manifests your dreams into reality while Archangel Ariel assists with manifesting your day to day needs.

Your Earthly material and financial needs can be received when you give it all to Archangel Ariel. Are you starting a new business? Call upon Archangel Ariel to join you during that process. Ask her to help you with getting you all the right tools you need to make it a successful business. This can be anything from the right office space to even business cards.

Archangel Ariel is nicknamed "Lion" or "Lioness" because she is often depicted as being seen with a wild animal with her or a Lion. She is strong and tough like the image of the Lion. If you say or think harsh words about yourself or others, Archangel Ariel can help you be more compassionate. She will be present with you when you need to be reminded of the messages of strength and courage. This has to do with your inner spirit and that you can accomplish anything you want to do. The Lion often seen with Archangel Ariel can be a symbol of the Ego, while Archangel Ariel is a symbol of the higher self. She always has complete control or domination over the Lion.

She is relaxed in holding the reigns of this wild beast. She does not put up a fight because she is strong and powerful. She does not ever need to push against any resistance, but rather glides right through it effortlessly. She does not fight or control the animal aggressively, but rather is assertive in her stance. She will remind you to own your life and be assertive.

Don't be afraid to say no if you are not interested in someone or something if it does not feel right. This is your life and you need to be the manager of it. Sometimes we may not realize when we are being aggressive over being assertive. The difference is that aggression is hostile while assertive is standing up for yourself without walking over someone. You will reach a place where you and everyone is else is respected and pleased with the outcome when you are assertive. It is far more effective than bull dozing over someone aggressively out of fear, anger or worry. We all do it at some time or another without realizing it, but Archangel Ariel will ask you to be mindful when you are behaving aggressively. When you are aware of it and cannot seem to calm down or stop it, ask Archangel Ariel to come in and channel your energies more effectively.

Archangel Ariel is typically seen with long flowing blonde hair and in complete commanding strength. I think of her as the sister of Archangel Michael as she is tough in her own right and presence. She says that we all have the power to accomplish whatever it is you choose. You must choose wisely of course, as vindictive power never garners Heavenly approval and support. Archangel Ariel can help you manifest your material and financial needs when you invite her into your life.

Archangel Ariel is a tough warrior female hierarchy angel. When you ask her, she can come in and assist you with magically manifesting your desires in steps. Need to improve your finances? Ask Archangel Ariel to help.

> *"Archangel Ariel, thank you for taking care of me in all ways and guiding me to the right home that is suitable for my temperament. Thank you for guiding me to a financially*

successful career. Thank you for working with me in ensuring
that all of my material needs are met and that all of my bills
are paid. And so it is."

Archangel Ariel is deep in our oceans, high up in our mountains and present in the open desert. Anywhere in nature is the best place to commune with her although you can ask for her help wherever you are. She is so powerful and unlimited like all Archangels, that she is everywhere at once. She watches over all of God's creations from animals, pets and our habitat. She steps in and intervenes with those who harm any of God's creations and protects our planet in the process. She does not take it lightly when human Egos inflict destruction on nature. Archangel Ariel is a fierce and powerful soldier Archangel that can infuse you with a fighter spirit and bring out your compassionate inner power helping you to obtain all of the wonders you've imagined in your dreams.

Archangel Haniel

ARCHANGEL HANIEL HAS A SOFT blue light around her which she uses to re-center and ground your soul. She communicates through your feelings and can assist you in awakening your intuition, as that's where the true answers live. She will typically show up when you need to be urged to withdraw from the noise of your daily life. Her energy is delicate and gentle. When she moves into your room or area it is often so subtle you might not notice it unless your clairsentience is running on high gear. If you're in tune to feelings and sensations of everything around you, then you will likely sense her presence.

Archangel Haniel works with artists and creative people opening up their sixth sense in order to assist them in producing exceptional work. When I am writing she moves into my vicinity filling it up with her bluish-white light. Her purpose is to keep me in a warm state of mind by having a crystal clear communication line to Heaven. Archangel Haniel can turn the cruelest heart into something beautiful and loving. She tends to show up around those who are experiencing accelerated spiritual growth.

She is connected to the Moon cycles and can help you manifest during the correct phases of the moon. Call on her assistance during the night of the Full Moon and ask her to awaken your inner perception and release toxic energy, people and substances. She will work with you in getting you to trust the Heavenly messages you are receiving. She will help you to follow your intuition, how to believe in it, how to nurture it and how to move forward with it. Awakening and protecting your psychic gifts are some of Archangel Haniel's specialties. She is a gentle Archangel for the sensitive and those with deep psychic gifts.

Archangel Azrael

ARCHANGEL AZRAEL IS THE "ANGEL of Death", but it is not as ominous as it sounds. He ushers and escorts the human souls that are crossing over to the other side gracefully. He heals those grieving over a death or loss of some kind. This can be a pain you're feeling over someone's death or the hurt over a past relationship. If you are living a toxic life, he can help remove those negative blocks getting you to change course towards a more spiritually minded path.

When my father passed away in November 2010, I found him in one of the rooms in his house on the floor. There were a couple of people frantically trying to revive him. Archangel Azrael was also there in the room when I walked in. I told them that my father had passed on already. Those around him were understandably in a panic shouting for him to wake up. It is difficult to speak to someone who is under stress as you have likely experienced at one time or another. I remained calm and firm, as I tend to be in most situations where others are not. I let everyone else react in ways that are typical when a death has happened. I calmly lit candles to bring in my father's angels.

Archangel Azrael came in and pointed to my father's heart. I nodded knowing that was the cause of his death. He had passed on in under a few minutes. It was a smooth transition process to the other side. My father was shown something profoundly incredible where the Light was. He experienced immense joy and serenity. It was enough for him to choose that peace instead of any discomfort and pain he was having in this life. The negatives he felt in this life such as stress caused issues to his body, but his soul was always kept in tact.

Archangel Azrael doesn't leave during this process as he comforts the grieving and those who have a tough time accepting someone's death. He is unlimited as all Heavenly benevolent beings are and can be everywhere at once. The death of someone we love is nothing to fear or be upset about. It's a natural part of life and is not truly a death. The body your soul inhabits has reached its maximum potential or that soul has fulfilled it's full purpose in this lifetime. Your soul can no longer reside in that body, but your soul itself never dies. It is the body that dies and disintegrates back into the Earth, but the soul exits the body and moves onto the "other side" or whatever you believe Heaven to be.

Archangel Azrael can be present for you when you are experiencing difficulty over the end of certain friendships or relationships. He can be with you as you end certain toxic lifestyle choices. At times you are being forced to end circumstances that no longer work for you. The conditions you were living in only stalled and held you back. This can be a work related endeavor or relationships including love and friendships. Many suffer through some inner turmoil during this process. Archangel Azrael will assist you in easing your heart so that you can have a peaceful ending with whatever it is you are looking to eliminate and bring to a close. Some of these endings might be forced and not what you had initially wanted, but they are necessary for your growth. They are essential in order to bring in brighter circumstances to you. You might experience a roller coaster ride of emotions including anger, depression and even forms of grieving when there is an ending of any kind in your life including a death. Call on Archangel Azrael to be with you and help you if you are feeling distress or grieving over anything in your life. He can help you unburden the load of heavy emotions associated with this departing, while guiding you through this transition in your life so that you can be at peace quickly.

Archangel Metatron

ARCHANGEL METATRON AND ARCHANGEL SANDALPHON are the two Archangels who were once in human form. They ascended into an angel due to the profound work they did on Earth. Archangel Metatron was the prophet Enoch in human form before he transformed into an angel when he crossed over.

As an evolving spiritual teacher through the course of my life, it is Archangel Metatron who has been there making sure I stay on my path. He guides me in the direction of contributing to help this world be a more beautiful place as he does with all spiritual teachers. He helps me stay balanced through giving and receiving gestures. He taught me that giving out assistance and the free wisdom to others in passing to be the same as giving. When no one else appreciates or notices what you do, he tells me it is all recorded in Heaven and that is all that matters. He helps you be more open to receiving. If you have trouble with receiving or have felt undeserving of anything ask him to remove those feelings and thoughts from you. He can remove those blocks and help you to see and understand how you are a child of God who is just as worthy as anybody else to receive. Do not allow yourself to experience guilt or fall into the space of feeling unworthy of anything good handed to you. To deny receiving is to create an imbalance in your life. If one side is lopsided you block manifestations and good things that the Creator bestows on you.

Archangel Metatron can help you balance your giving and receiving energies and get your life on track. He will guide you to organize and prioritize what is important. He will lead those who are ready to become a more evolved spiritual soul. Archangel Metatron records the good and bad things you do in a book. This is the book that is pulled out when you cross over for your life review. He is the Archangel who steps in to guide sensitive children helping them to stay on path and become a spiritual warrior of light. If you are new spiritual teacher you likely have called in Archangel Metatron in to your life without knowing it. Receive him and his wonderful gifts and knowledge in the right spirit. He is also the Archangel that can manipulate time and space.

Archangel Sandalphon

ARCHANGEL SANDALPHON IS THE OTHER Archangel who once lived as a human soul. He was the prophet Elijah. Archangel Sandalphon works with tender energies and is the angel of music working with artists of all kinds. If you are a singer or musician you would do well to invite Archangel Sandalphon into your life to assist you in making harmonious music. He aligns my clairaudience with the messages I hear over the notes and sounds of music.

He bridges the gap linking the physical Earth with the spiritual heavens. He can help you stay connected, grounded while being linked to Spirit. He helps with your ascension in deciding whether you are ready to move to the next spiritual path or not. He is a super compassionate archangel, which is why he tends to show up for the ultra sensitive as to guide them gently out of heightened turmoil.

Archangel Sandalphon will often stretch appearing taller than a human soul can comprehend. He will stretch his body from Earth to Heaven bridging both worlds. He reminds us that all of our wishes, dreams and hopes happen through Divine timing. You must first complete one step, before the next one is shown. Call on Archangel Sandalphon if you have been using harsh words towards yourself and ask him to infuse gentleness into your life. If you are a singer losing confidence in your voice, ask him to pour his turquoise light energy into your throat Chakra. If you have major prayers you feel are not being heard by God, ask Archangel Sandalphon to step in. He delivers these great prayers to God for immediate answering.

Archangel Raguel

ARCHANGEL RAGUEL IS INSTRUMENTAL IN harmonizing relationships of all types, whether it is friendships, love or business connections. If any discord arises with your relationships with others, ask him to help you balance, elevate, smooth and mend the connection. Fighting injustice, wanting harmony and a fair resolution are other areas in which Archangel Raguel can assist you. You cannot get away with treating others badly as Archangel Raguel will come in and correct your behavior.

One thing to note is that Archangel Raguel will not get rid of a love interest you are having trouble with, but rather will enter the situation to help you see it in a new light that benefits everyone involved. This is not the case if your significant other is abusive, but rather when misunderstandings arise with no hope for solution. He rushes in to infuse his light in the situation by merging both of your souls to a place of understanding and love. Do you have to deal with difficult co-workers or a tiring parent? Ask Archangel Raguel to restore balance and harmony on this and other situations where you are experiencing discord.

Archangel Chamuel

ARCHANGEL CHAMUEL HAS BEEN OFTEN referred to as, *'the finding angel'*. Archangel Chamuel can help you find anything from the right career, love partner, home or even your keys! I have had incidents where I am frantically looking for something I misplaced. I stop remembering to ask for help. *"Archangel Chamuel, please help me find...."* Almost immediately I head straight to where the item I lost is. I will hear him clairaudiently tell me where it is or he will tell me claircognizantly—where I suddenly just know exactly where the item I misplaced is.

If you are in the middle of a career or job transition, ask Archangel Chamuel to be by your side ushering this change. He will help make the transition effortless and smooth ensuring that you are moving into the right work position. He also works with the Romance Angels when someone longs or wishes for a loving, soulmate relationship or new friendships that are more aligned with your beliefs. He will only bring you those that are positively beneficial to you. If your twin flame is living in this lifetime with you, he can assist you both in uniting while having the courage to speak to one another.

He is present sparking new passion into current relationships and married/committed couples who are experiencing issues. Before you can attract in a new career or partnership, it is first important to love and believe in yourself. Archangel Chamuel is all about the love and can infuse God's love into a cold heart. He will awaken your heart Chakra if it is blocked and help you to attract in love. Call upon Archangel Chamuel if you need help finding the right career, job, love partner and friendships.

Archangel Zadkiel

ARCHANGEL ZADKIEL IS THE ANGEL of knowledge who will walk by your side if you are a teacher, student of higher learning and spiritual pursuits. He can keep your ear Chakras clear of debris so that you can clearly hear the voices of God, the Guides and Angels. He can assist with helping you remember things you need to know from grocery lists to speeches you need to make publicly. Writers can work with him if they are writing a book that contains tons of information that is easy to forget. Call on Archangel Zadkiel if you need help with unloading heavy toxic burdens and if you need to experience mercy, compassion, help with forgiveness or letting go of past pain.

Archangel Jeremiel

ARCHANGEL JEREMIEL COMES FORWARD TO do your life review with you when you cross over to the other side. Contrary to some beliefs of you being judged by God, you do go through a life review where you may find you judging yourself for your actions on Earth. This is why it is important to face what you have done in this lifetime. Look at what you have been through in the past and heal those wounds that others caused to you or where you inflicted hurt on them. Make your peace with it now. Archangel Jeremiel will assist you with this when you let him know that you are ready.

In my book, "*Reaching for the Warrior Within*", Archangel Jeremiel was front and center guiding me through my past so that I could forgive and let go of what had happened. This was in keeping only the lessons and love that led me to where I am today. I did a serious evaluation of my life and the experiences I went through personally while writing that book. Doing this helped me remove former patterns and ways of living in order to move to the next spiritual plateau and see life through new eyes. The purpose of a life review with Archangel Jeremiel is so that you can correct your mistakes so that you do not continue making them. He prepares and ushers you through and toward positive transformations in your life. Ask Archangel Jeremiel to help heal and release past pain in your life while ushering you into a brighter new world.

Jesus Christ

*J*ESUS CHRIST IS NOT AN Archangel, but he is one of the most powerful benevolent and compassionate beings in the Heavens that I felt compelled to mention him. It was important that I include him as he has been a huge significance in my life at times. I knew who Jesus was and had learned about him going to Bible School as a child. The images of him are everywhere around the world in Churches and people's homes. I have been privy to the negative words by those who claim to speak the word of Jesus. I have heard those same negative words by those who do not believe. It can be rattling that one man can cause such harmful thoughts in others.

I had avoided him at all costs until he came in during a spiritual reading I did for someone one day. Jesus came into the room with me with immense force. It flushed through me and awakened every pore and cell in my body. I felt lightheaded and was prompted to pause as my head fell over. When I adjusted to his energy I experienced an incredible feeling of love that I had ever felt before. I didn't want it to end. I knew him as if I knew a friend without question or suspicion. I discovered the person that I was reading for was praying to him daily for healing. Jesus was coming in to reassure her that he is hearing her prayers. He was working on healing her ravished heart.

You have all likely had a crush on someone at one time or another. You know the feeling of that crush where it's a roller coaster ride of excitement and immeasurable happiness. Now magnify that feeling by a million and this will give you a good idea of the feeling Jesus Christ conveys when he is with you. He is a magnificent love light and you experience it all over and around you. The tears you form are tears of joy as he has the power to blast away any negative emotion or block just by sitting next to you. You feel a vast greatness that prompts you to be moved to tears.

I learned two things about Jesus that I was previously unaware of. He is all about love and healing in a grand way that I never knew or understood. No one ever talks about that and that bemuses me. What I have personally heard or been privy to were lines or statements condemning and disapproving of other people. I have never received that impression when I have connected to him. In fact, the Jesus that comes in is someone other than how they have described that I wonder if they know him at all. He is a powerful healer and can work with you to have trust and faith in the miracles working for you in your life. His healing is done through this overflowing feeling of love that you may feel dizzy. It is as if you are soaring above the clouds with joy. His presence is so intense and massive that it is impossible to forget.

Jesus said that his messages have been mistranslated over the centuries. It reached a point where they have now been so poorly interpreted that it is no longer his message. His message of course is simple and on par with all of Heaven and that is love. His main goals are always revolving around love, compassion and healing. My Guides and Angels continue to tell me that this Earthly run is all about learning to love and express love. Jesus only emphasized this with me when he came in, as he is the King leading the pack.

Jesus Christ is profoundly psychic and was as a man on Earth. He was one of the biggest healers and prophetic teachers we have had in history when he was living. Jesus was and is giving, compassionate, otherworldly and full of love. There are good people in every group, but in my research and in the media, I've only been privy to the negative words that others vocally shout when it comes to Jesus. This is why so many get uncomfortable when I say the word *Jesus*, because of the negative connotations associated with the word. His name has been so inadequately portrayed in the media by both sides of the debate that I have no idea who they are talking about. I have found that others I have met shutter at his name. When I speak of him, I speak of him because I know him personally. I have met him and communed with him. He has the most astonishing presence as a spirit that ever graced the Universe and the Heavens together. I admire and adore him.

There are religions that teach that your soul will be trapped in your body when you are buried if you have not accepted Jesus Christ as your personal savior. There are people that believe that some of us will burn in hell and bonfire. None of this is true to my findings. According to God's law they are free to live and speak as they choose even if it is not true. No one has had any experiences to report back regarding this alleged damnation. Whereas there are many who communicate to the other side who have received and reported countless accurate information regarding a stranger's loved one. They relay information to that person about their loved one that is accurate. I have spent my entire life experiencing first hand of what the truth is by conducting my own communications with the other side. The helpful information being fed to me ends up coming true. This was how I grew up and there is no other belief system that can or will ever sway me. Discover the answers for yourself by doing the work and not living in fear.

Jesus wants you to work on being a good person always striving to improve yourself and do the best you can to operate from a place of love. I don't respond to any other source no matter what they claim. It has no bearing of truth to me and nor will it ever. I do not act purely on faith and trust which is why Heaven had to spend so much time in my life convincing me. When I started seeing and experiencing results, I knew that they and it were real.

We have heard stories from others that have said that Christ is coming or that they are the Coming of the Christ. Christ is not coming and nor is that person the coming of the Christ necessarily. Jesus Christ is one of the most powerful spirits in the Heavens now. He can be with every one of us at the same time if we ask him to. What I have been told by him is that Christ is not coming because he is already here. Due to the fact that he can be with so many people at the same time, he is also living in many of us. He is unlimited in that pieces of his soul exist in certain people. These are the people who do the work of bringing others together, who teach about love, who teach about humanity and compassion. These are the people who live in this space and are doing his work because they are channeling him often unknowingly. He is not coming in the way others have guessed in creating a hole that swallows up mankind. He is already here in many of us doing HIS and God's work.

The coming of the Christ is already here and we are all around you. Some of you may not even be aware that you are doing his work, but you agreed on it before you arrived. Live as Jesus did. Love yourself and your neighbor. Work together in healing one another and this world today.

Epilogue

Human souls often choose to live in fear and obsess over power and control. In this state they infuse their lower self into the Holy print in the name of God. They paint false pictures to control others through guilt and fear. This is what they consider to be a moral way to live at any given time in history. The only ethical range that exists is your own character. You are here to make your own choices and decisions as to the best course of action for yourself. When you make a poor decision you pay for that consequence. Every time you get knocked down you are experiencing a lesson. Each lesson you learn helps you to grow to be a smarter and stronger soul. God and the angels will never stop loving you. It only pains them to watch you suffer needlessly. They see no need for you to exude anger and other wasted emotions and feelings that have no positive power over anything in the end. Those feelings are reactions that your Ego objects to. The only true power that exists and overcomes is God's LOVE. Keeping our Ego quiet is up there on one of the most difficult tasks for us to do. We're human after all and born with these Egos that we wrestle with daily. We have these Egos in order for us to learn necessary lessons that assist our soul in growing and evolving.

How many times are you going to allow yourself to get knocked around before you wake up? When are you going to grow up and be fully aware of your actions, your thoughts and how you treat others? When are you going to learn right from wrong? When are you going to learn to love unconditionally? When are you going to learn to treat others with respect?

The best way to quiet your Ego is by stating positive affirmations that all is as it should be and everything is taken care of for you. Even if you do not see your desired outcome yet, you need to act and believe as if it is already here. You need to live in a state of gratitude and feel joy for this life you have been given the opportunity to have. Do not let someone else's Ego stop you from your purpose and goals.

When you look back on your accomplishments you may have noticed that they came to you when you were not struggling for it. It came to you naturally and effortlessly. We all want things immediately. There are reasons that your desires are delayed or are not instantaneous. Some of the common suggestions the angels urge us to have are patience, trust, faith and love. Try living in this state every second if you can. Practice it regularly and do this especially when you know you are being tested like when you get a flat tire and you're late for work.

Do you ever notice that when you push for a relationship to happen with someone that it ends up back firing and not going as planned? This is because you cannot push for anything including love. As far as love and relationships go, those that merge blissfully are when both of you are patient allowing it to evolve on its own course.

In order to improve your life the first thing you will need to do is reduce or eliminate your addictions, bad habits and even some friendships! When you ask your heavenly spiritual guides for assistance you may be prompted to make crucial life changes that you may not feel ready to make. They have you do this because you are being prepped for something greater up ahead. Before that can happen, you will have to strip away all of your toxic baggage. You may be absorbed in it to the point that you might not be aware that it is poisonous. They do not ask you to do this because they are against the fun you have when you have an alcoholic drink. They do it so that you can live a more blissful life full of happiness, success and love. They know that vice is only a temporary high that is not long lasting and delays you from moving forward. You're too busy battling the side effects from your addiction to have enough energy to focus on what's important. When you continue on with your former toxic way of living this gets in your own way of success and holds you back. You may remain stuck at a dead end job you do not want to be at. When you have all that poor energy around you it blocks good things from entering your life.

This is about stripping down to your soul core and eliminating particular behavior patterns and lifestyle choices that are disruptive to your soul's enhancement. It can take some time dissolving these things, as the changes do not happen immediately. They will be met with some resistance or unhappiness. You are shredding all of the bark around the tree that is part of your life experiences, so that your true inner light of God shines as bright as the sun. Once this is done then you will be shown your next move. This can be digging up those projects, ideas and anything you have always wanted to do, but were stopped by procrastination or negative self talk. You will attract in friendships and relationships of a higher caliber on your new improved level. You will stand in your own power with great strength and there will be nothing that you cannot do. The flood gates open for you to tackle and accomplish your dreams. When you get started the universe will meet you tenfold!

At the time this was written and complete around the holidays, I connected with Mother Mary and Jesus Christ for any messages to incorporate in here. The message they gave me was to experience joy now. Joy has been hammered home all throughout this book. I know for some of us that might seem like a difficult place to get to. There are things that you can do to elevate your feelings into a happier state of mind. Do something fun with a friend. Surround yourself with other people who lift your mood. Watch a comedy or a lighthearted, feel good movie. Blast some good music. Stay away from negative substances that will only bring your vibration down. These are things such as news headlines or going out to places when you know it's going to be packed tampering with your energy.

I am out there in the trenches with the crowd's everyday so I get it. I temporarily placed myself in a part of town that borders soulless on purpose. You could call it research or just plain crazy. I witness harsh energy regularly. I conduct frequent sessions of shielding every day because of this. I am careful with what places I head to, what time of day it is and who is around me. The morning before Christmas Eve I witnessed many people rushing around frantically and unhappy. They were pushing and shoving each other aggressively. Some were even getting into fights that were taped on cell phones of onlookers. Others waited until the last minute to shop since their heart is not in it or they are functioning with no time and energy.

A friend of mine who was out there as well called me to ask, "What's going on with everybody?" People have lost sight of what is important. They are hurrying around doing what they feel is expected. The only thing you should be doing is getting back into the joy of your life. Regardless of your spiritual beliefs, it is unavoidable to know that the Christmas word is meant to be a time of joy. It is the kind of joy you should be reaching for daily. You should be celebrating! You should be celebrating this life and each other.

Remember what is truly important to your soul and why you are here. It is to love, to give and to spread love. This mantra should be adopted everyday and every minute of your life. Deep down your soul knows what you can do to bring yourself back. Know your light. Know your power. Know what you were born here to be. Be one with the Light and one with Spirit. They are waiting to walk beside you, in front of you and with you. They see us all holding the hands of our neighbor no matter what they are into or what they are like. If you treat your neighbor without love, then you don't know God. When you see yourself and others with disgust, then you only know the Ego and the Devil.

Love is who I am. Love is the source of all that I wish. Love is the source of power. The more that I love, the safer I am. The more that I allow myself to love the more powerful I am. Sending god's light and love is not enough. It is powerful and necessary. Some of us have a soldier nature in the name of Heaven and we do have to fight. When I say fight I don't mean with violence, but by being assertive in our stance. We have to stand in our own individual power. Think and speak for ourselves even if we stand alone. All of our goals are to unite as many people as possible in peace, love and joy.

Have zero tolerance for anger, violence and hate, which gets everybody nowhere. Yet we cannot be a doormat either and nicey-nice all the time. There are some of us who are specifically here to exude the characteristics of love, which warms the coldest of hearts. We are an army of workers of the light who all have varying and specific gifts to contribute to ushering the world gracefully into a new age. This is why we elected to show up at this time in history. This is how we all found each other. It's all connected. We are all connected. We are soldiers and fighters of the light. We are warriors in the name of God and Heaven. I am a warrior of light and I exude the honor that God desires. Join me in teaching this message so that we can shift and change this world for the better, one person at a time.

Questions From Readers About Spirit Guides & Angels

Q: *What is the best way to contact guides when you are having trouble connecting through meditation?*

A: Spirit Guides and Angels are by your side the instant you call them. You do not need to do any special invocation or meditation to communicate with them. The reason why meditating is effective is because it puts you in a calm and relaxed state. You are more apt to receiving their messages clearly when you are in that space, rather than stressed or distracted.

Q: *Can you explain blinks of light? I've been seeing them for years. Not sure if it is guides.*

A: There are angel trails or lights that may show up in one's peripheral vision if the third eye is opened up. If this is the case, then you are seeing them clairvoyantly. They do appear as lights for some people.

Q: Do guides work through numbers to get your attention? When you see the same sequence of numbers could it be your guide?

A: Angels and Spirit Guides communicate with us in many ways and yes through numbers and symbols is one way.

Q: With meditation, how do we know if we are connecting with our guides and it's not our imagination or wishes?

A: They will use the pronoun *"You"* while our own thoughts and Ego use the pronoun *"I"*. Your higher self is 100% psychic while your lower self is not. We all communicate with them in varying ways, but mainly through our 'clair channels'. If you are receiving positive messages and nudges repeatedly, then it is likely them. These messages will come to you more than three times. Our Ego or lower self will conjure up something once and discard it. If your Ego is being repetitive or 'obsessing', it is prompting you to do something that you know is not good for you. The messages or guidance from Spirit will be urging you to do something that will benefit you or everyone involved positively.

Q: Could Children's imaginary friends be Spirit Guides?

A: Children are more adept at communicating with Spirit Guides. They don't hold lower self judgments the way we as Adults have learned to do. Children know more about acceptance and love than any adult. Adults are damaged Children who were lured into a certain way of thinking due to their surroundings and upbringing. Children view things in a purer way and use less of their Ego. The Ego blows up to the size of a football field once Adults get a hold of it.

Q: I'm new to this, what are guides?

A: A guide is a spirit on the other side who is assigned to you through the duration of your lifetime on Earth. Their purpose is to help, nudge and guide you along the right path steering you away from wrong choices if you pay attention to them. They do not make your decisions for you, but they do intervene when you are going off course. They are essentially your right hand confidante who knows everything about you including your thoughts, feelings and needs. They do not help you fulfill needs that are against your greater good such as hanging around the wrong people, doing drugs or being absorbed in addiction. In fact, they nudge you to steer clear of bad vices. Our Ego is so powerful that it often ignores the wisdom your guide has for you.

Q: When I meditate I see faces of people I do not know. Are these guides?

A: They may be your guide or an angel, but not always. You may be outwardly projecting your subconscious mind. This may prompt your mind to display shadows. This is a form of clairvoyance though.

Q: How do you tell the difference between a Guide versus an Angel?

A: A guide is typically someone who had an Earthly life, but went through advanced training on the other side to be a pure Spirit Guide for a human soul during its Earth life. Guardian Angels were never human in my experience, but always a spirit. They may appear human for you to avert you from danger or crises and then disappear.

Q: Can guides heal you with your body and mind?

A: Some have specific specialties that they work with you on like love, health, career, etc. They heal our body and mind so that we are operating from our higher selves and more able to communicate with God.

Q: Are we able to call more than one Guide for help with different projects or problems? Is it always necessary to call them?

A: You can call on as many Guides and Angels as you like. When they have worked with you on a specific issue and there is no need for anymore assistance, then they leave. Your main Spirit Guide and angel are always around you and never leave. They guide and help you along

215

your life path. However, it is necessary to call them, as they cannot intervene with our Free Will unless we have asked them to.

Q: *How long do you experience meditation before you feel your guides' presence?*

A: To feel them it can take anywhere from 5 to 15 minutes of meditation or by being still and relaxed. Breathing is important as it not only relaxes you, but delivers oxygen into every cell in your body allowing you to be a fine tuned receptive communication tool with them. It's like clearing the static of a telephone.

Q: *I get those voices that tell me what's going on. It's a voice, a feeling and a twinge in my heart area all at once. They validate questions at times, sometimes they validate before I have the questions. Is that my Guide?*

A: If the messages you are receiving this way end up coming true, then yes they are your guide or your angel.

Q: *Do the deceased watch us do things like taking a shower?*

A: They do not watch us shower, dress or have sex. They do not have that kind of attraction or interest. They see our souls as lights and feelings. If that gives some of you peace of mind to know you're not being watched every time you strip down. Those on the other side are not Peeping Tom's. The only exception may be an Earth bound spirit who chose not to cross over and is basically hanging out in limbo mode. They get a rush of re-enacting the same activity with a human soul indefinitely until they make the move into the light to be purified.

Q: *How can I find out the name of my Spirit Guide and Guardian Angel?*

A: Knowing there name varies from person to person. There are times where they do not go by any name, specifically your guardian angel who has never been in human form. Some may make up a name so that you feel more comfortable able to address them in some way. It doesn't matter how you address them. You can ask them to tell you there name. Ask them to continue to show you signs and confirmation of what it is. Then start paying attention to the signs and symbols in your surroundings. Perhaps in the following week or so you keep running into people with the name of "James" and you see that name out of nowhere on Billboards, signs etc. That's one way they can communicate with you.

Q: How do I communicate with the Archangels?

A: Communicating with the Archangels happen the same way you communicate with the angels, guardian angels, spirit guides and deceased loved ones. Being in a meditative state helps since it puts you into a more calm and receptive place. When you are calm and feeling uplifting joy without any chemicals is the most efficient way. This is when your energy vibration is raised closer to Heaven and you receive divine communication effortlessly and clearer. When we are under stress, experiencing negative emotions, or on heavy alcohol, bad foods or other toxic vices, then this creates restrictions, which form blocks that clog up these etheric phone cords that connect us to Spirit. Of course they are always communicating with us, but are we hearing them?

Q: Why do people who do bad things or hurt others have great success in life or seem to have it easier? How come those who do good get nowhere?

A: One of the things is that some of these perceived bad people know they are going to get what they want no matter what. Their intention to getting what they want is so great and they are so optimistic and sure of themselves about it that they manifest it. They are not going to get away with something bad. If they do, it will be short-lived. They will be stopped. The angels see the goodness in ALL people whether that person is good or bad. They do not place them into separate categories. There are guides and spirits who are not Egoless and are doing different work in Heaven. They see the behavior of mankind and do not take it lightly. Each individual case would have to be examined to give you the reasons why as its not that cut and dry. If a good person is not manifesting, but instead living in frustration over it, then that is what they are attracting to themselves.

Q: I am starting to open my heart and eyes to new vibrations and I am trying to have a connection with angels by just sending them my love. The more I do this I seem to be getting small white feathers left in front of me. At work, home in the street even one in my hair. What's going on or am I starting to be weird. It's almost daily now. I'm not sure what to do so I feel happy to pick it up and say thank you? Should I be doing something? Well I think I have made myself look strange enough for now but I had to ask someone and it's not something I can bring up around people I know.

A: That's not strange or weird at all. You are opening yourself up more to the light and to the angels. When someone is making an attempt to communicate or connect with the angels sometimes they wonder if they are being heard. Some of us don't visually see the angels in front of us and so we may question whether or not they are hearing us. The angels have connected with you the second you have put out the intention to communicate with them. They try various ways of making contact with us back either through our various senses or in other ways through numbers and symbols. It's how we communicate with each other.

We have various ways of communicating whether by phone, email or texting. Since they can't just pick up the phone, they use divine ways of communicating as we will too when we cross over. We won't need things like phones or computers. One of the big ways that angels like to let us know that they are hearing you is they love to drop white feathers around us. You suddenly start finding them in places where it doesn't seem feasible for it to suddenly show up. They tend to do it quite a bit with those who are fervently trying to connect with them. They will do it when someone is desperately needing an answer to something specific and wondering if they're being heard. You are. This is their way of telling you, *'we hear you loud and clear'*. There is nothing you need to do, but accept this love that they are showering upon you. You can even save the feather in a special place as a gift if you choose.

"Thy word is a lamp unto my feet and a light unto my path."
—Psalms

Let your Spirit team of God, Angels and Spirit Guides
be your companions on your life's journey.

Available in paperback and kindle by Kevin Hunter,

"REACHING FOR THE WARRIOR WITHIN"

Reaching for the Warrior Within is the author's personal story recounting a volatile childhood. This led him to a path of addictions, anxiety and overindulgence in alcohol, drugs, cigarettes and destructive relationships. As a survival mechanism he talks about splitting into different people who took over and ran the show for him. He credits turning his life around, not by therapy, but by simultaneously paying attention and following the messages he has been receiving from his Spirit team in Heaven since birth. He explains how he was able to distinctly tell the difference between when his higher self was intervening and ruling the show and when his lower self was running his life into the gutter.

Living several lifetimes in one, he did not let anything stop him from getting his life together, going after what he wanted and getting it. He explains how he pulled himself up by his bootstraps and obtained every job he wanted without prior experience. This is from work in the entertainment industry with some of Hollywood's respected talent, to ridding himself of toxic addictions, and living a healthier lifestyle clear minded.

Kevin Hunter gains strength, healing and guidance with the help of his own team of Guides and Angels who navigate all of us through the treacherous waters in our lives. Living vicariously through this inspiring story will enable you to distinguish when you have been assisted on your own life path.

Reaching for the Warrior Within attests that anyone can change and do it if they pay attention to their own inner guidance system and act accordingly. This can be from being a victim of child abuse or a drug and alcohol user, to going after the jobs and relationships you want. This powerful story is for those seeking motivation to change, alter and empower their life one day at a time.

About Kevin Hunter

KEVIN HUNTER is an author and love, dating relationship expert born with piercing insight into the human condition which he receives through clairaudience and claircognizance cues. His books tackle a variety of genres and tend to have a strong male protagonist. The messages and themes he weaves in his work surround Spirit's own communications of love and respect which he channels and infuses into his writing and stories. His books include the self-help inspirational book, *"Reaching for the Warrior Within"*, the horror/drama, *"Paint the Silence"*, the young adult dating guide, *"Dude 101"* and the modern day erotic love story, *"Jagger's Revolution"*.

Before writing books and stories, Kevin started out in the entertainment business in 1996 becoming actress Michelle Pfeiffer's personal development dude for her boutique production company in Santa Monica, California. She dissolved her company after several years and he made a move into coordinating film productions for the big studios on such films as *"One Fine Day"*, *"A Thousand Acres"*, *"The Deep End of the Ocean"*, *"Crazy in Alabama"*, *"Original Sin"*, *"The Perfect Storm"*, *"Harry Potter & the Sorcerer's Stone"*, *"Dr. Dolittle 2"* and *"Carolina"*. He considers himself a beach bum born and raised in Los Angeles, California.

Visit www.kevin-hunter.com